Praise

'Dani has brilliantly summarised the most important principles of franchise marketing into a comprehensive and easy-to-follow system. This is a must-read for any franchisor looking to grow a strong and engaged network. I now keep the Five Fs of franchise marketing on my desk to make sure I am always aligned with my strategic goals.'
— **Jenny Farenden**, Franchise Marketing Director

'If you want fifteen years of condensed franchising experience in one book, this is it. Dani shares her experience and knowledge in a phenomenal way, setting every franchise up for success and holding your hand along the journey!'
— **Jennifer Hadjieva**, Business Consultant

———— FOREWORD BY ————

RUNE SOVNDAHL, FANTASTIC SERVICES CO-FOUNDER

FRANCHISE
FAME

An insider's marketing guide to incremental growth and soaring success for franchisors

DANI PELEVA

Re think

First published in Great Britain in 2022
by Rethink Press (www.rethinkpress.com)

This book is dedicated to my family, who have been with me throughout my journey and have always showed me unconditional love

With best
wishes,

Davi
Peleve

Contents

Foreword

In this world of constant change, being independent is getting harder and harder. As technology evolves and competition gets fiercer, franchising is the way to remain independent and still have the power of partnership – between brands, systems and entrepreneurs who want business success, without all the hassle and uncertainty of that business being a startup.

Franchising as a model relies entirely on people. As a franchisor, you need to select the right people to work with, as well as the right partners to join you along the way. Enabling people to achieve their business ambitions is what the real reward is for me. We are on a mission to help a thousand people become successful franchisees and make their first million.

Ever since we founded FantasticServices.com back in 2009, I knew that it would flourish. I envisaged thousands of people connecting under the same brand, the business going global and having hundreds of thousands of happy clients across the globe. Little did I know that this would be done through franchising. But once we decided to go down that route, it all made perfect sense.

To create and run a successful franchise, you need to recruit and grow the franchisees. That can sometimes be a challenging task, especially after you have dealt with all the formalities of the franchising process – the legal matters, the creation of your franchise playbooks, manuals, and other supporting documents and systems. At Fantastic Services, we created the Fantastic Academy to support all who join the Fantastic family with a vigorous and comprehensive onboarding process and ongoing training programmes. Continuous learning and development is at the heart of our culture.

Naturally, we faced the challenge shared by most franchisors: lead generation and how to spread the word about how fantastic our franchise is. This is where Dani and Franchise Fame came in. I have known and worked with Dani for more than twelve years now. She's always had a curious and critical mind, and I liked her can-do, practical approach. Back when we were a startup, she would say, 'This is the problem – let's solve it', and she did.

Over the years, she headed our marketing and branding departments and continuously displayed that same passion and character. There was no task or project too difficult or impossible for her. I knew that I could trust her to move mountains for us. Dani was intrinsic to the development and growth of Fantastic Services and as a company, we wouldn't be where we are without her. She owned a Fantastic franchise herself and championed a new service, which was a storming success and is still part of our portfolio.

In this book, Dani has distilled and described the key principles of franchising. Her model, the Five Fs of franchise marketing, unpacks more than a decade of value and experience in this sector. Whether you are new to franchising or have years of experience, this book will give you a tried-and-tested, step-by-step guide to successfully grow your franchise and reach new territories.

In a global marketplace where there are so many franchising opportunities, how you stand out and market your business is crucial. *Franchise Fame* provides a clear and comprehensive method on how exactly to do that, in a sustainable way, and involving every person in your business. Because, after all, franchising is all about people.

Rune Sovndahl, serial investor, entrepreneur, business mentor and co-founder of Fantastic Services

Introduction

As a franchisor, you provide the much-needed structure and support for those who would like to start their own business but haven't got the experience or confidence to do it alone. This means that you must possess the business acumen and ambition to not only support your franchisee network, but to grow and take it to the next level, expanding into new cities, countries and even continents.

Franchising as a business model is continuously gaining more traction among aspiring entrepreneurs. A lot of the literature out there talks about the franchisee and their decision-making process, such as how to select the best franchise to invest in and so forth, but little is said about the franchisor. This book is for you.

Franchising your business is proof of success on its own, but it also marks the start of a new and exciting chapter. If you have franchised out your business, chances are that you have a lot of knowledge and experience to share with your network of franchisees, including best practices to put in and the worst obstacles to avoid. But perhaps you have also fallen into traps you never thought existed, and you sometimes might feel out of your depth.

Working closely with franchisors for over a decade, as well as being a franchisee myself, have helped me identify those traps and common pain points. I have been involved in digital marketing and franchising for more than twelve years now. I know the industry inside and out. I've been where you are, and I fully understand the three major pain points for most franchisors.

The first problem is that you feel your franchises are invisible. You have spent years developing an idea, turning it into a successful enterprise, and then franchising it. You have attended to legal matters, created the operation manual and franchise agreements and implemented a pilot franchise scheme. So it's incredibly frustrating to find that there isn't a long queue of prospective franchisees at the door.

Competition is fierce. Franchisees are often drawn to organisations that claim to have found the formula for success, even if there's no proof this is the case. It's simply not a level playing field. Franchisors that have a sound business model and a great product but don't have a clear marketing plan and strategy aren't able to attract entrepreneurs.

The second problem is that you struggle to get a stream of good-quality leads. To succeed, you must identify potential customers, but are unsure of how to do this. As a result, you often use unqualified in-house or agency teams who can't deliver. On top of this, traditional franchise directories often send irrelevant leads that go nowhere. This leaves you confused and frustrated, after you have already paid extortionate rates.

The third problem is lack of time. On a daily basis, you have to handle finance, marketing, communications, and more. Working extra hours at the weekend becomes the norm. Your packed schedule means you have little opportunity to focus on developing a franchise network.

These problems combine to make you feel that you can't make progress, and you are making sacrifices both personally and professionally for seemingly no reason. *Franchise Fame* addresses these pain points by providing a proven methodology and solution to each of them. The five-step model used in the book, also called the Five Fs of franchise marketing, provides a holistic view of franchise marketing and how to use it to achieve growth and success without sacrificing your work–life balance. This method offers a tiered approach to bringing the different aspects of your business together towards the common goal of achieving franchise fame.

Often the solution to an initial problem causes other problems to emerge. For example, you may hire someone to help with franchise recruitment, but the new recruiter picks the wrong candidates for partnership, because you lack a clear idea of who your ideal franchisee is. Or maybe you invest your entire budget on lead generation without supporting your franchisees with top-level marketing activities. There are many books and guides about franchise marketing and lead generation, but they fail to bridge the gap between franchise growth and all participating parties in the business model.

This book addresses that gap. It will give you more clarity about the key mistakes that are made in franchising, help you identify and break repeating patterns, as well as provide deeper understanding as to how marketing can be used to facilitate growth in a cost-effective and efficient way. I also share best practices and case studies involving big names in the industry that have implemented the Five Fs of franchise marketing method and achieved national and international expansion.

My method has been improved and refined over my years working with franchisors from around the globe. Despite the different markets, core business activities and audiences, there is a common thread linking successful franchisors. They find the right formula to effectively scale their business while maintaining a healthy and productive 360-degree relationship with everyone who touches their business – their franchisee network, head office team and clients, who happily become loyal to the business. This book and the Five Fs of franchise marketing will help you achieve that too.

PART ONE

SETTING THE SCENE

One of the reasons why most franchise marketing efforts fail is because of a lack of a structured methodology. This section of the book gives an overview of the Five Fs of franchise marketing and explains who this model is suitable for. It also tells the story of my journey in franchising and marketing and to what and whom I owe my drive and passion.

ONE

Foundations

My journey in franchising started without planning or knowing where it would take me. All I knew was that I had a curious mind and was fascinated by business and entrepreneurship and wanted to know how people become successful in life. Since then, that curiosity and hunger to always learn more have continuously helped me to exceed even my own expectations and to achieve ambitious targets that I once would never have believed I was capable of. Franchising felt somehow logical after a series of events in my professional and personal life, alongside the conscious choices I made. This chapter details my franchising story and the discoveries I made by playing different roles in the franchising model.

Where it all began

I often get asked to what I owe my passion for business and, franchising in particular. Reflecting on my childhood, I realised that it comes from a key moment in my past. I grew up in a small town nestled in the mountains of Bulgaria. Times were tough and my parents' teaching jobs were hardly enough to support the family. They had to work two jobs to make ends meet, often coming home after 10pm, completely exhausted. This is what drove them to start their own business.

I was still a child, not more than nine years of age, when my parents tried to become entrepreneurs themselves. It was my responsibility to look after my younger sister. I would deal with the housework, cooking, cleaning and doing the washing, because of the long hours my parents had to work. They were trying to start their own luxury furniture manufacturing company. Sadly, it didn't become profitable and had to close a few years later.

They had had a great product that they did not know how to get on the market. They knew next to nothing about scaling up and growing a business, managing and mitigating risks, recruitment, and so forth. The stakes were too high – they couldn't lose their full-time jobs – and they did not have the time or knowledge they needed to dedicate to their own venture. Looking back, if my parents had been given structure and support, similar to what franchising offers, they may well have been successful. Unfortunately, they were on their own.

Inspired by this experience early in my life, I have always found business and entrepreneurship fascinating. More specifically, helping businesses grow and succeed excites me and makes me feel accomplished. Through helping others' enterprises, it is almost as if I am helping my own parents' business thrive.

Starting up in business

When I joined Fantastic Services back in 2009, the company was a startup and hadn't even considered franchising out. I had just finished my postgraduate degree and had moved to London without much of an idea about what I wanted to do. All I knew was that the world of business excited me, and I knew very little about it. From then on, it was a journey with many unexpected turns and obstacles I had to navigate to prove my worth, grow internally, and lead a team to help the brand get to where it is today – a global franchisor with hundreds of units worldwide, which continues to grow into new territories. It wasn't easy, but it was a lot of fun.

At first, the startup environment of managed chaos, lack of hierarchical structure and flexibility worked miracles for the brand. We quickly scaled up from two employees to 500 in less than a couple of years. Those days were swamped with tasks, calls, quick decisions to be made and executed. I'd wake up and jump on a conference call and then turn around and look at my watch and it would already be seven o'clock in the evening. Working weeks were often sixty to seventy hours long, but the passion and drive we all had were relentless. It was mainly because we were part of the process of creating something new that we could see growing and developing into a business, which would later on provide work opportunities for thousands of people around the globe. It was fascinating to be part of that experience.

A few years down the line, we were faced with serious challenges, such as lack of commitment from the contractors we worked with. It was difficult to maintain the same quality standard across all of them, the job scheduling was often compromised and so was brand consistency. Once the company decided to go down the route of franchising, it was a game-changer. The structure solved a lot of underlying issues the company had with its contractors, vendors and even clients. It took a while for us to apply the changes and adapt, but we all knew we were heading towards the common goal set by the CEOs – global expansion.

I was tasked with looking after all marketing and branding initiatives for the UK market. That meant speaking with franchisees on a daily basis, making sure they adhered to all branding guidelines, running onsite inspections, surveying customers, even visiting clients with the franchisee teams and overseeing the process of delivering the service. I was also in charge of strategising and executing online and offline marketing campaigns to generate leads for the network and keep franchisees content, while staying on top of the company websites, organising photoshoots, liaising with the sales team about active promotional offers, and many other tasks I do not even remember now. It was a deep dive in marketing and franchising, an invaluable learning experience, and the foundation of my career.

A few years later and hundreds of franchise units sold, I decided that I had plateaued and needed to get back to university. My then-partner quit his nine-to-five and we bought a Fantastic Services franchise. I spent the next couple of years working on my master's and managing a franchise that quickly grew to twelve teams on the road. I then clearly saw the other side of the coin, being a franchisee in the organisation – the struggles, the pains and problems, as well as the rewards of working for yourself and being your own boss. Running my own business, while not feeling isolated like many startup founders do, that was the environment I needed to learn and grow.

Graduating from UCL was one of the best decisions I had ever made. Having academic and practical experience allowed me to match all the pieces of the puzzle and not long after, the idea was born. I identified a gap in the franchising market and my next business venture was to head Local Fame, a global franchise marketing agency. Working with dozens of franchisors from six different continents has helped me gain deeper understanding of the franchising model from all perspectives – franchisor, franchisee and vendor. It is from this understanding that I was able to develop the model of the Five Fs of franchise marketing.

I also identified the three key challenges faced by most franchisors:

1. Brand visibility

2. Finding quality leads at a reasonable cost

3. Time management

The consequence of all these isn't great. You become stuck in operations, sustaining the current low number of franchisees but not growing the business, accompanied by the feeling you are not making any progress at all, sacrificing personal life and time spent with loved ones for something that doesn't even feel like success. And this was definitely not what you got into business for in the first place. To make things worse, there is the occasional franchisee who wants to close down, and a new buyer must be found, otherwise your business will shrink rather than grow. These things happen, right?

You end up feeling like you are trapped in a vicious circle and there is no way out. You are working the hardest you have ever done, and the results are still not as good as you'd like them to be. Frustrated, helpless and exhausted are the first things that come to mind when someone asks you how you are. Instead, you respond with the usual: 'I'm fine.' If that sounds familiar, this book is for you.

This book provides a holistic solution to all three of those pain points. They can be frustrating, but the very fact you have made it this far, and are reading this book, means you have the bandwidth to go on and continue to work on your franchise. Now is not the time to give up. The Five Fs will give you a model that addresses all aspects of your business and will help you achieve your goal of growing your franchise, without having to break the bank or sleep at the office and risk burning out. It is possible, believe it or not.

Shifting your mindset

But first things first, before moving on to the actual solution, certain commitment from you will be required. You will need to shift your mindset for this model to stand a chance. Perhaps you have already tried out some solutions and they haven't worked. You neither have the energy nor the time to begin to try out new techniques and hypotheses.

I completely understand. I've spent the last ten years of my life practising and proving this formula, so it is not hypothetical at all. Franchisors have tested this model in the UK, Central America, Australia, Central Europe, the States and many other locations. Regardless of the size and industry the franchise was in, my method worked its magic without exception.

All you need to do is approach the method with an open mind. Ignore every negative experience you have had so far, and just let those five founding principles of the model sink in. Visualise how you can adopt the advice in the following chapters and put it into practice in your own business.

I have always been a fan of critical thinking – my team can easily confirm that – but try not to criticise any of the Five Fs before you have read through all of the chapters. As the ancient Buddhist proverb goes, 'Always keep an open mind and a compassionate heart.' You may feel some or all of the five principles of the model are already implemented in your business, but there is always something new to be learned.

It is important to know that if one of the principles is not applied, the whole model becomes dysfunctional. All Five Fs are there for a reason. Omitting one leads to imbalance in the model and affects its efficacy. Only when all five attributes of the model have been considered and worked on, will the model be sustainable and lead to long-term success.

At the end of each chapter, you will find a summary of the key takeaways. Scattered throughout the book are also links to downloadable resources that will help you apply the principle of the model in your franchise. Part Three of the book looks at sustaining the model and applying it on a global scale. Once you have completed the book, you will also discover a small gift at the end of it, so keep your eyes peeled.

Summary

- The model serves as a solution to the three major pain points franchisors often experience.

- Keep an open mind while going through the book and the model. There is always something new to be learned.

- If implemented only partially, the model becomes dysfunctional.

TWO

The Promise

Now you know why I have written this book, the next logical thing to look at is who and what it is essentially about. In this chapter, I shall share an overview of the Five Fs model and will explain how it engages everyone involved in your business.

Who is the Five Fs model for?

The Five Fs is a methodology that provides a solution to the most common problems around marketing your franchise. Franchising as a business model unites a wide number of stakeholders. Franchisees, partners, vendors in the supply chain, the franchisor and their head office support team, and of course the clients, are all integral to the business. They work in collaboration and synchronisation under the specific franchise brand. Understanding this franchising ecosystem and the roles inside it is crucial for success.

Much has been written about franchising, usually focusing on lead generation, franchise sales and expansion. The literature often fails to address how all players in the franchising model engage and work together to achieve success. Very little attention is paid to you, the franchisor, and your team. This book aims to break the pattern. We'll view franchise marketing through the lens of management, looking at how to manage all key stakeholders in parallel for sustainable growth and soaring success. The Five Fs are also suitable for anyone involved in franchise senior management, such as operations and marketing managers and their teams, as the model clearly defines how your specific business objectives can be achieved, what steps to take and what parts of the business to focus on.

I strongly encourage you to share this book with your team and use it as a platform to build a solid franchise marketing plan, one that encompasses all parts of and participants in your business. Once you have identified all the key players and have considered their roles in your plans, you will clear the path to be able to achieve your goals.

Whether you are just starting out and are on the lookout for your first pilot franchisee, or you have sold dozens of units and are now considering global expansion, the model and principles of the Five Fs are applicable to your business. The only difference is that if you are early on your franchising journey, you have the unique opportunity to get it right first time and save yourself hundreds – even thousands – of hours on suggestions that do not work, are costly and only leave you disappointed and frustrated.

On the other hand, if you are a franchisor that has tried and tested everything out there and are on the brink of giving up, do not be discouraged. Your efforts were not in vain. You have learned lessons, as uncomfortable and expensive as they may have been. Once you go through the Five Fs, the principles and suggested action plan, it will all suddenly click, as if you have always had this knowledge but just never put it into practice.

That's right – the actual model does not suggest anything new, nor does it reveal a striking truth that you have never heard before. It is highly likely that you will have come across some of these ideas. But what is innovative about this model is the way it aligns all parties in your franchise. It puts each one under the spotlight and stresses the pivotal roles they play in the growth and success of your business. As the conductor of that perfectly synced orchestra, you have to manage, organise, facilitate and mediate for the magic to happen.

What do you need in place before you begin?

If you have already identified with one or more of the pain points described in the previous chapter, your franchise has a problem that needs solving, and the sooner you address it, the better. What is needed, as trivial as it may sound, is your acknowledgement that something needs to change. Only then will you be able to trust the process and follow its implementation. Over the years helping franchise owners challenge those pain points, I've noticed that only the ones who acknowledge that they are not hitting their goals or are facing challenges in their franchises actually go on to succeed. Realising and admitting to yourself that your business is not growing at the speed you'd like it to, or that you are challenged by a particular task and actively seeking help with it, is the starting point for growth. As you learn and seek help to develop, so does your franchise.

Repetition is the mother of skill, as the saying goes, so even if you have heard of some of the principles of the model, keep an open mind and think about what more you can do for your business to add value. Ask yourself whether you are missing out on something, or how you can improve what you already have in place. Most importantly, trust the process. It has helped hundreds of franchises around the world hit their short-and long-term targets and become successful.

Change often feels uncomfortable and counterintuitive. Our brains will tell us to stay in our comfort zones and not to take any unnecessary risk. But once you have admitted that you need to change something to steer your business in another direction, it becomes easier to follow the advice.

Last but not least, have faith in yourself and the team around you. You will not be able to do it all alone. Gather people around you who will support your focus, ambition and dedication, and who will encourage you to sustain the results achieved and keep going. Positive change does not happen overnight, and consistency is the key to success.

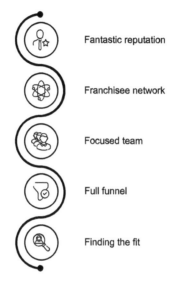

The Five Fs of franchise marketing

What are the Five Fs of franchise marketing?

The Five Fs of franchise marketing each correspond to a role in your business. They are:

1. Fantastic reputation

2. Franchisee network

3. Focused team

4. Full funnel

5. Finding the fit

Let's look at each of these in turn.

1. Fantastic reputation

Your reputation precedes you. It puts your end client on a pedestal – without your clients, you are out of business. What they think about your business, how they engage with it, talk about it and review it online are of major importance to the success of your franchise. Your reputation is one of its biggest and most valuable assets, and it is something you should never overlook or mismanage.

Building a business reputation is something that takes time and effort, but it is worth the work. Businesses these days thrive not just because they provide products and services in and of themselves, but because these products and services are ones that their customers appreciate, remember and love.

It is highly unlikely that if your franchise's reputation is poor, you're going to be growing in revenue and expanding to new locations. The opposite is more likely to be true. Prioritising your brand's reputation will add value to your entire network by increasing conversions – and therefore revenue – and decreasing marketing expenditure. What's more, your franchisees will thrive, which means better returns for you. Most importantly, potential franchise buyers will be able to look at your company with the confidence it deserves.

2. Franchisee network

A business never operates in isolation. There are customers, vendors, employees, etc. In franchises, there are even more key relationships to take care of, as there are 'partners' involved in the business process, whose success means your success. Meanwhile, their challenges can cost you a lot over the long term – whether in reputation, finances, time or resources. This is why investing in your franchisee network is crucial.

An underperforming franchisee signals that something in the mechanics of the franchise is not functioning optimally, or perhaps the franchisee lacks motivation or the right attitude. Whatever it is, you will need to look at the problems in a deeper way, try to resolve the situation and not let it get out of hand. After all, this could mean loss of reputation, leads, revenue, and potentially the franchisee altogether, which would leave you in a sticky situation.

Then there are the franchisees who perform well. What lessons have you learned from them? How are they applying the business model you've set out and what steps are they taking to ensure their full compliance with your rules and methods of service delivery?

This second principle of the Five Fs asks you to create the space for frank conversations with your franchisee network, to take tangible steps to improve the franchising process, and to facilitate this development on an ongoing basis.

3. Focused team

Burnout and exhaustion are the most likely outcomes of trying to handle all the franchising tasks in your business yourself. It is essential to put resources in place to avoid stretching yourself too thin, including implementing a support team. In this day and age, when there's a wide talent pool of specialists available, and at competitive rates, it's a no-brainer.

This third principle of the Five Fs is dedicated to the team around you. These specialists are specialists for a reason – they can take on a task and get it done in a few hours, when it would have taken you twice as long. Being able to delegate tasks will also free you up to tackle the other challenges that come your way.

A simple addition of one person to your team can make a world of difference in terms of how you do business. For example, a personal assistant could take care of most calls and emails, while you attend to the crucial meetings with franchisees. Or you could hire an external company to take care of some of your marketing tasks for you. Them being experts in the field means you don't have to be a master of all trades. Hiring the right individuals for the right skill set frees up more time for you to focus on what really matters

– your higher priority tasks – allowing you to strike the right balance when it comes to moving your business forward.

4. Full funnel

Every franchisor wants one thing for their business, and that's growth. Whether that's in the form of new areas being developed or new revenue streams, that lead to royalties paid by franchisees, this is where your priorities should lie. The last two of the Five Fs are dedicated to attracting and selecting the right partner for your business for maximum growth.

Your activity needs to be laser-focused if you're to succeed with your growth plans. Essentially, this means not spending money on broad campaigns that don't target the right individuals. Creating a solid buyer persona or customer avatar (or a number of these) will help you home in on your ideal franchisee. It's easy to think that anyone can be a franchisee and that no experience is required, but that's hardly ever the case.

Once that's done, you'll be ready to tailor your campaigns directly to this buyer persona. You can lead them to your web pages, you can create ads – anything as long as you've got a strong call to action that either puts them in direct touch with you or enables them to leave their details for you to contact them. Remember to think like your ideal buyer: they'll have questions that you will need to answer as clearly and concisely as possible.

Then there are the metrics. You'll need to analyse whether your campaign worked, then use your findings to improve your strategy and fine-tune it so that it yields even better results in the future. This way, you'll fill your funnel with quality leads that get you somewhere, instead of shooting in the dark hoping for results.

5. Finding the fit

They say, 'If the shoe fits, wear it', but what happens when the shoe doesn't fit? It might seem like an oversimplified way of looking at things, but this philosophy applies to franchising, too. It essentially boils down to the fact that you need to recruit new franchisees to grow your business and revenue, but not every person will be suitable for this process.

After filling the funnel with the right potential individuals, with whom you'll be developing a long-lasting relationship (think five to ten years or more, as this is the standard for a typical franchise), you need to make sure they're actually the correct person for the business. You should do this through a carefully designed and developed lead qualification process. Then, once you have found the right fit for your franchise and have gone through the legalities and signed the documents, a very important step follows: training.

The onboarding of a franchisee is as important as the selection process. When developing your training programme, you need to make sure that you design it as well as you've designed the most fundamental part of your offering – that which caters to your customers' experience. After all, if your franchisee is unable to offer high-quality standards of service to your customers, this could affect the service offering itself, your business's reputation, the other franchisees in your network, and more.

For a successful and fruitful partnership, it's vital to choose franchisees who can live and breathe your business model and are just as excited about it as you are.

The Five Fs in practice: The Fantastic Services story

During my time with Fantastic Services, we focused on continuous improvement, as we knew that through getting better at what we did, we would be able to accomplish our bold expansion plans. First and foremost, we understood how important it was for us to collect positive client experiences in the form of reviews and display those on our own media pages, as well as third-party platforms, to cultivate a positive brand image and reputation. This helped us retain existing clients and attract new ones, which kept franchisees content.

We also focused on local marketing initiatives to generate phone calls and bookings for the franchisees and keep them busy. We had mastered that to such an extent that whenever someone searched for *'cleaning Angel'* or *'handyman Chelsea'* or *'plumber Watford'*, Fantastic Services would be top of the searches. We were just on it, no exceptions. That helped us build an incredibly strong relationship with our franchisees and have their constant support and trust even at the toughest of times. On those grounds we could ask them to perform better, improve their service, train their staff further, and much more.

The head office was growing exponentially too. To achieve all of this, we needed a talented and creative digital marketing team who championed Google searches, Google Ads and social media. We recruited and hired the best web developers to build websites that converted leads into paying clients, and built a diligent franchisee management team, who helped with all internal comms. Without those backend teams, the company would have stood no chance of achieving the growth we got. Our franchise opportunities sales funnel was always full, thanks to the landing pages and lead generation campaigns we continuously worked on. We knew exactly who we wanted to attract and what opportunities to offer.

A separate team was looking after the franchise recruitment and the lead qualification and interview process. Once a deal was signed, we'd pass the new partner to the franchise training and development team, who over the years developed a platform called 'Franchise Academy', full of useful content and onboarding videos about the organisation.

We all worked as one, like a well-oiled machine, because we all knew what our roles in the business were and what we were expected to contribute. But it is important to note that we did not get it right from the start. There were many failed attempts, frustrations and setbacks. It took us years to make this work. And only years after, reflecting on my past experience while creating the model, it struck me. I was having my eureka moment! Your franchise would only be successful if it ultimately achieved the Five Fs: fantastic reputation, a focused team to support you, a network of happy and successful franchisees, a funnel full of high-quality leads, and a process in place to find the right fit of partners to join the network.

I had the opportunity to try out the model almost right away. In 2013, I was sent to Melbourne to work on a three-month project. The UK side of the Fantastic Services franchise was doing exceptionally well, but the Australian master franchisor not so much. Since I knew the business inside out, the CEO asked me to go down under and implement everything I had learned that had led to success back home. It was a great opportunity for me to put the Five Fs model into practice. I'm not going to lie – it wasn't easy, as I found myself in a completely new environment. Economically and culturally, things were not the same as back home.

The first thing I did was to rebuild the head office team. This had been an underlying issue for months, and it was impacting the whole organisation. I focused on interviewing franchisees and spent time with their teams on the road to analyse the way the actual service was delivered. With small adjustments and training for the existing franchisees, we improved the client retention rate dramatically over a period of three months. This meant a higher number of happy clients, lower rate of complaints, better reviews and improved reputation. The franchisees appreciated having someone speak to them, discuss and address their needs and make small changes to the sales and marketing process to make their work easier.

In the third and last month of my time there, I focused entirely on setting up a better training programme for existing franchisees and an onboarding one for new ones. We converted the ground floor of the office building into classrooms where we could teach training courses and make sure every new selected partner underwent a thorough qualification and onboarding process.

After only three months of implementing the model, the Australian franchise had dramatically improved sales revenue, retention of existing franchisees and new units sold. It was a record quarter. The model was an absolute success for sure. The master franchisor reaped the benefits of that success and continued to maintain the model. I returned to London, where I was commended for successfully completing the project and thanks to that, I earned a promotion that same year. Not long after, the franchise sold its first units in Queensland and Western Australia.

Years later, and after working with dozens of global franchisors who have implemented the Five Fs of franchise marketing, I can confirm that the model works without exception. Applying the model in your business will give you the chance to expand into new territories, hit ambitious targets, and exceed your own expectations. You'll be able to rely on a steady supply of new leads, and won't need to be involved in the process. This will allow you to spend more time at home with your family, while still growing your franchise network, keeping your current franchisees happy, and fulfilling the day-to-day requirements of your business.

Summary

- The Five Fs of franchise marketing are:
  - Fantastic reputation
  - Franchisee network
  - Focused team
  - Full funnel
  - Finding the fit

- The model has been validated numerous times and it works without exception, across different markets and industries.

- The model unites all participants in the franchise in achieving the common goal of sustainable growth and soaring success.

PART TWO

THE FIVE FS IN DEPTH

Now you know what the Five Fs of franchise marketing are, it is time to take a deep dive into all five key elements of the model to fully understand them. We'll look at practical examples of how they can be applied in your franchise. Each of the following chapters prompts you to take an action or promotes an activity you can undertake right away that will facilitate implementation of the model later on. Packed in the next few chapters, you will also find case studies of real businesses I have worked with and the impact that the Five Fs model has had on them.

THREE

Fantastic Reputation

L ike every other business, a franchise relies on sales and generating new customers. Your reputation and the way your end clients review your services can either make or break your business. Ensuring your franchise has an impeccable online reputation is only the first step in the process, but it is a fundamental one for achieving franchise success.

How to manage your reputation

A buying decision is influenced by a number of factors, of which reputation is one of the most important. Studies show that a quarter of a company's market value can be directly related to its reputation.[1] Also, 68% of potential buyers are happy to pay a premium price if they know that the service or product they are buying is of high value and quality.[2] When cost and availability are equal, often the decision to purchase is swayed by the reputation of the brand – or in other words, what your customers say about you. Reading reviews of clients who already tried and tested your brand is often the way new customers make a decision before they commit to buy. If those reviews are negative, you will probably end up losing that lead to a competitor. It is highly unrealistic to expect your franchise to grow if its reputation is poor.

It is a common misconception in business that if it delivers a good service, its reputation will be good too, without having to pay attention to it. While this is partially correct – if you do a good job, your clients are likely to be content with your product or service – leaving your quality score in the hands of your clients or franchisees, without at least monitoring it, is not a great idea. Happy clients are a lot less likely to write a positive review for your brand online, whereas angry customers will want to make sure they tell the whole world about their poor experience and make sure nobody else is let down like they have been. Forbes reports that 94% of consumers avoid a company

1   Deloitte & Touche, *Global Survey on Reputation Risk: Reputation@Risk* (Deloitte & Touche, 2015), www2.deloitte.com/content/dam/Deloitte/za/Documents/risk/NEWReputationRiskSurveyReport_25FEB.pdf, accessed 13 February 2022

2   Gladly, *Customer Service Expectations Survey: Trends and insights from consumers about customer service* (Gladly, 2018), www.gladly.com/blog/2018-customer-service-expectations-survey, accessed 13 February 2022

with bad reviews.[3] The same study suggests that one negative review can drive away around 22% of leads. One bad comment about your business could cost you dearly.

For example, let's say your customer lifetime value – in other words, the amount of profit your average customer contributes to your business over the duration of their relationship with your company – is £1000. One of your franchisees has had a bad day and makes a mistake with a client. That can happen to anyone, right? Or perhaps they had an unreasonable client. (We all have those from time to time.) That client decides they will write a huge negative review for your business across all platforms, to make sure nobody ever makes the same mistake of using your services. Twenty potential clients of yours see the review and as a result, decide to use somebody else. That single review would have cost you £20,000.

This situation could be easily avoided if the customer's review was attended to. A small compensation, a refund or a voucher, for example, could be worth it to prevent you from losing the greater amount of other customers' business. Looking at it in this way really puts things in perspective, doesn't it? Why would you spend money on marketing only for people to see a negative online reputation and not convert their inquiries into sales? Having worked in digital and franchise marketing for more than

---

twelve years now and most of it on the agency side, I can say with a high level of certainty that all our clients who have improved their online reputation have seen a dramatic increase in conversions without having to up their advertising or marketing budgets.

Think about the last time you searched your brand online and checked your customer reviews. When was that? I would strongly advise doing this often – at least once a month. Check platforms like Trustpilot, Feefo, Checkatrade, Facebook and Google My Business. Do you see any patterns? Are customers appraising the same thing or criticising another? This could be anything from being late for a service to not cleaning up after yourself once you have delivered the service, or perhaps not greeting them the right way when they enter your shop. Small things like that can make a huge difference.

Are some franchisees performing better than others? Are some locations generating happy client testimonials and others not? What is your average rating per location or franchisee – how many stars? That is a great key performance indicator (KPI) by itself. If the answer is under 4.5 stars then you should reconsider the reputation management strategy adopted by your franchise. Ideally, you should have an average rating of 4.5 stars or over to make sure you don't lose any leads to competitors because of what clients are saying about you online. After all, you have probably spent a lot on attracting those leads to come and notice your brand, either through advertising or marketing, running campaigns, organising events and paying for ads. Losing them at the end of the sales funnel rather than converting them into a paying customer would be such a waste of effort and resources.

If you or your franchisees have any negative reviews, you are now probably panicking and wondering what to do with them. While improving your franchise's online reputation will take time – positive change does not happen overnight – the good news is that you can heavily influence that process.

What is online reputation management?

Online reputation management is the action of monitoring, overseeing and influencing what your customers say about each of your franchisees and your franchise brand on all platforms possible. There are ways to do that in a structured and methodical way and this section looks at those ways in detail.

There are ways to encourage clients to review your franchisees and leave positive comments that will eventually increase the overall reputation score of the business. This can be done through sending automated emails requesting customers to review your services and encouraging them to do so through organising raffles and giveaways. The use of a Customer Relationship Management (CRM) system here is helpful. Once you know a service has been delivered, an email should automatically hit the inbox of your customer asking them to review you. By doing this, you also show you care about your business and how it is perceived by customers and that you are always looking to improve. And if any of your franchisees has made a mistake and done poorly, at least you can find out first before the client goes on all other platforms complaining and destroying your reputation. A CRM system costs nearly nothing to set up but it provides valuable intel about how your network of franchisees is performing and at the same time safeguards the reputation that took you years to build.

You could also get your franchisees to leave a flyer or business card with their clients asking for a review. Incentivising your clients with something as little as 20% off their next purchase if they reviewed you, for example, would mean you get their appraisal (hopefully) and you encourage them to become a return client. Or your franchisees could deploy a slightly different technique and give something complimentary while the customer is still with them, along with a QR code that takes them to somewhere they can easily leave a positive review. After all, we all like freebies, don't we?

The options, especially online, are limitless. But if all this is too much of a burden, you could always hire an agency to manage your online reputation for you.

How to respond to negative reviews

Generating the positive reviews and comments is only one step of the work, however. Once you receive any review, it is of essence that it is answered as soon as possible. If you are using an agency or have delegated this job to a person internally, using a set of template answers to positive reviews is standard practice. But negative reviews should be handled with highest priority, utmost care and with a custom approach. It is a must that they are responded to by the business. This not only shows to other customers that you value their opinion while looking after the reputation of your franchise, but also that you are down-to-earth and know how to handle a complaint in a timely manner on the rare occasion one takes place.

Here are some tips on how to do that:

- Always try and empathise with the client.

- Do not ever take the review personally. I know you care about your business, but the goal here is to stay calm and manage the situation professionally.

- Aim to take the conversation offline. Provide an email or a phone number for them to contact you on and discuss the matter further, or ask for their contact details so that you contact them and provide a solution.

- Keep a neutral or, even better, positive tone of voice while replying to their review.

- Say you are sorry that they have had this experience. An answer like that does not admit liability but shows that you are being empathetic.

- Suggest compensation of some kind – a refund, voucher, or whatever you deem possible once you have had a private conversation with the client.

- Inform the customer about any changes you have made in response to their complaint.

- Once you have rectified the situation, ask them to remove the negative review, or to write a new, positive review to reflect the resolution you have reached.

Remember, a negative review is not the end of the world and it is entirely manageable. Your unhappy clients can actually be your greatest source of learning. If you separate yourself from your emotions and don't take it personally, you can learn a lot about the weaknesses of your business and, best of all, you can change it for the better. By listening to customer complaints, you can spot the repetitive concerns, which should show you where to focus your next points of action in your overall process of continuous improvement. Positive outcome can be achieved by making incremental changes to the business and its operations over time.

Your franchisees are your reputation ambassadors

It really is not as hard as it sounds. Spending some thinking time and building a process is all it takes. You only need to do this once, but the business benefits continuously. Your franchisees should also be sold on the idea – the better their reputation is, the higher their conversion and revenue. It does not cost much to organise, apart from a couple of automated emails and someone in charge of responding to reviews online.

Your franchisees are your brand and reputation ambassadors. Training them on how to deliver exceptional customer service while looking after their own reputation and making sure they generate positive client reviews is essential for their business to grow, not to mention the overall success of the whole franchise. If you'd like to go one step further, you could introduce a Fantastic Reputation award and have a franchisee win the award every month, quarter and annually to further stimulate them to perform well. Perhaps you could highlight the best reviews the business has received in your internal franchisee newsletter and commend the franchisees who generated them.

Having your network understand the importance and value behind having a fantastic reputation is key to ongoing success. The company culture should be customer-centric and the whole network should know that their ultimate purpose is to be of service to their customers. Because if there are no customers, there is no business either – it's as simple as that.

Reputation and franchise recruitment

The reputation of your franchise brand is not only important for potential customers. It also influences stakeholder perceptions about your brand. Some of those stakeholders could be your future partners, ie, potential franchisees. Poor reputation will inevitably influence their decision when considering investing in your franchise or in a competitors' one. This is another major reason why you need to manage your reputation and encourage a customer-centric approach throughout the network.

One of the greatest benefits of the franchise business model is that franchisees are driven by the power of vested interest, which is why they are more likely to deliver service excellence than employees. But it is also up to you, the franchisor, to make it absolutely clear what the expectations are, to define and monitor the service standards to guard the reputation of the brand.

CASE STUDY – OVEN CLEANING FRANCHISE

This reminds me of the time when I owned as many as twelve oven cleaning franchise units. Business was going well, but occasionally we'd get a negative review that a technician had not cleaned after themselves or had left grease marks on the kitchen floor, or that clients were not completely satisfied with the level of cleanliness of their appliance. Because of that, they'd rate us with three or four stars rather than the maximum of five. This was simply not good enough, as our overall quality score was being impacted, and I wanted to deliver a five-star service without exception.

It took me a while to solve this one. I kept wondering what we could do better. I took some time to read all the reviews we had online. I even visited a few of the jobs with the technicians to observe the process, and then the idea was born. It was so simple! All we had to do was to introduce special protective sheets that the technicians would lay in front of the oven to protect the floor while working. Not only that, but we came up with customer inspection forms that we printed out, and later on even integrated into our CRM system. Every technician would ask the client to inspect their work at the end of the service and sign the document confirming they were satisfied with it. We would then ask them to review us by following a link in an email that they would receive as a follow-up.

The measures we put in place dramatically reduced our complaint rate and increased the number of five-star reviews we received, as well as our overall rating. The technicians were also very happy, as they'd get tipped for the great customer service. It was an absolute win-win!

WANT TO KNOW MORE?

Download our e-book on franchise reputation fail examples to get an idea of what it can cost your franchise if you do not manage your reputation carefully. You can find it on www.franchisefame.com/book.

Summary

- A brand's reputation has a direct impact on its sales conversions.

- Negative reviews can cost you up to 22% of lost potential customers.

- Your franchisees are your brand ambassadors.

- Training your franchisees regularly improves your customer service and reputation.

- You need to actively manage your reputation – assign a person/team/agency to do so if you can't do this yourself.

- All client reviews should be answered, especially negative ones.

- Other stakeholders are affected by reputation. Good reviews reassure potential franchise buyers to invest in your business.

FOUR

Franchisee Network

Franchising is all about building relationships. Relationships with your team, vendors, franchisees, clients, and everyone who touches the business. If one of those relationships is imbalanced or dysfunctional, your franchise suffers the consequences. This chapter looks at the importance of having a strong network of franchisees.

But before we take the plunge into your network and evaluate how successful it is, 'success' first needs to be defined. We should all agree that a franchise is only successful when its franchisees are. Some franchisors measure success by the number of franchisees in their network, others by the revenue that they generate per franchisee – although this often fluctuates per location, as some franchisees make more money than others. Success is subjective and needs to be defined when setting clear business objectives for the quarter, the year, and in your longer-term business plans.

Your franchisees are the living proof of your business success. If they struggle in business, this probably means that your franchise is also in trouble. Assuming that you are already an established franchise, chances are that you already have some challenges with underperforming partners. Think about the franchisee who struggles to hit targets – why is it that they feel challenged? What doesn't work in their favour? Every franchise has that franchisee who struggles with sales or has another problem that makes it difficult to grow in revenue and, respectively, profit. I am certain that you have at least one franchisee who always calls you to complain how difficult it is for them to make their royalty payment for this period, how business is sluggish, sales are down. Do you often sigh when you see an email or a phone call from them, as you know what the conversation is going to be about?

Can you relate? This chapter looks at what can be done about this so that you stop having those difficult and negative conversations with your franchisees.

Managing underperformance

When you first come into an agreement with your franchisees, you shake hands on them investing not only in a territorial unit but also in your business, support and knowledge. If you fail to provide any of these, it is likely your franchisees will struggle. A franchisee who feels alone and unsupported is a recipe for disastrous business performance – negative attitude arises, the way the service is delivered is affected, the number of unhappy clients increases, and that in turn creates reputation and brand damage. Then the number of franchise leads also drops – after all, nobody wants to invest in a poor business with many complaints. The franchisee feels even more alone, neglected, deceived, and loses trust in the brand and in you as a franchisor. This means any guidance and directions from the head office will not be adhered to, as the relationship between both parties has been destroyed. To make matters worse, this may lead to the franchisee wanting to exit your business, so that you have to close a location or resell it.

On the contrary, imagine a healthy relationship with all of your franchisees – a scenario where they take on board everything that you recommend, follow the best practice guides and fully adopt the strategy of the head office. Over time, their performance improves, and so do their revenue and profits. Not only does this translate into more royalties for you as a franchisor, but the happy franchisee network feels accomplished and successful. They overachieve on their targets and become strong ambassadors of your brand for outsiders, being living testimonials and proof of your business concept. Most importantly, they then help turn potential franchisees into new partners in your franchise model.

Talk to your network

You may now be wondering how to put a support process in place, so that you end up with successful franchisees. There are a few ways to go about it, but it starts with having honest conversations with your network. Setting up regular quarterly or monthly meetings, and a franchisee committee of top performers who actively help in decision-making, is one way to draw upon the expertise in your business community. The top-performing franchisees have a story to tell, and it is a good idea to involve them in planning. You could have the committee convene every quarter and discuss strategy for the next one, as well as vote on certain topics, share experience and help you in some of the operations, training and onboarding of new franchisees. Encouraging peer group meetings where the top-performing franchisees can share experiences and give advice to newer franchisees can also do wonders.

Set up a system

If you have an underperforming franchisee, how do you evaluate where the problem is? Do you listen to sales calls? Do you use a mystery shopper? Or do you just have a chat with the franchisee themselves? Identifying the reason why they are underperforming can be a challenge, but it could mean that they need additional training, or some more leads in the sales funnel, or that they are going through a tough period in their personal life and just need someone to talk to. Regardless, your role is to analyse, identify and solve the problem.

It's a good idea to have a system in place to identify the first signs of underperformance. Setting clear KPIs and measuring them regularly can help you do this. Those KPIs can include sales revenue, number of new clients, average client lifetime value or retention rate, depending on the industry your franchise is in and the nature of the business. But whatever they are, it is important to keep track of those metrics and have a minimum target that all franchisees need to hit. Once someone drops below the minimum threshold, your support process should be triggered, to investigate the reasons why the franchisee is not performing as well as they should be.

Create a checklist

A checklist may come in handy to explore all aspects of the business that may have led to the underperformance. There may be an issue with sales, operations, recruitment, customer service or any number of other challenges that I am sure you would have had to deal with yourself at some point when you were growing your business. Your expertise here is needed more than ever. Think critically about what has gone wrong or may go wrong in your business and unpack your ideas in a document. This will be the foundation of your checklist. Use this in a review meeting, either formal or informal, to get your franchisee's input and find out where the problem is. Follow up with regular review meetings, where you ask them how they are doing and give your franchisee feedback on their performance.

Marketing your franchise

You should manage your franchisee network proactively rather than reactively. Why wait until a franchisee starts idling? Why not instead ensure they are all doing great and even exceeding expectations? You can do this by using the marketing fund in a cost-effective way that provides equal opportunities and return on investment for all franchisees.

Onboarding a new franchisee and letting them run their business as they like is not acceptable if you are looking for long-term growth. The concept of franchising is fundamentally about replicating success and continuous support, building a strong network of franchisees and putting processes in place to facilitate their practice. Having a marketing fund is one small step of the whole process, but not enough on its own. Without a solid franchise marketing plan, the fund will not go a long way. You need to use that fund for the benefit of your franchise network.

Do not forget that collecting contributions from the franchisees towards their marketing is a responsibility on its own – you are accountable to the franchisee and you need to prove their contribution is being used to their best advantage. I have worked with hundreds of businesses over the past decade and in many cases, franchisors were criticised by franchisees for misusing the marketing fund, taking the wrong decisions on how to spend it, or not bringing a decent return on investment from it.

Some franchisors believe it is entirely up to the franchisees to market themselves locally and will only spend on lead generation to sell new franchise units, because they see an immediate return on investment for every new sale. By doing this, they fail to see the bigger picture – namely that investing in your franchisees will also bring a great return on investment long-term. In other words, if the franchisees are successful and are generating higher revenue, then the franchisor will be collecting higher royalties. What's more, if your franchisees are thriving, they become ambassadors of success and of your brand, and potential franchisees are easily swayed into investing in your franchise.

Local marketing and Google My Business

Because franchising is about replicating a business model in a particular geographical location, marketing your franchise locally is essential to its success. There are a number of ways to increase brand visibility in the local area, from business directories to leaflet distribution and radio and television ads. But nothing is as effective as having a solid online presence in local search results. Launching a local marketing campaign for each of your franchisees is a great way to ensure that the business is always discovered by potential customers and their sales funnel is always full.

Much like the paper business directories back in the days, Google has created its own free business directory, where every locally based business can register for free. It is called

Google My Business and is a fantastic product for franchisees who need local presence or for any business with a physical location.

Google My Business offers a great opportunity to increase the online visibility of your franchise. The level of flexibility it offers is wonderful and you can input detailed information about the products and services you offer, working hours, business description, location and contact information, images, and many more. Depending on the sector you are in, Google My Business allows further customisation. For example, you can upload food menus if you are a restaurant, or select from a list of pre-defined facilities such as swimming pool, car parking, accessibility, etc, if you are a hotel. It harnesses local searches and, based on the information you have input for your business, presents users with business results in their area. Those local searches can be anything like *'cleaning Chelsea'*, *'hairdresser Fulham'*, *'Italian restaurant Prahran'* or *'dentist West Palm Beach'*.

Your Google My Business listing can be a powerful lead generation tool if used correctly. People search for products and services online on the go, from the comfort of their home or at work. Google picks up their location from the GPS signal of their device and uses this to show them the top two or three providers near the place where the query was made. The ultimate value for your Google My Business listing is for it to appear in those top three results, so that potential clients can discover your business and come into contact with you.

Get to the top

In the last decade, there has been a spike in *'near me'* searches for people searching for a business on the go. Anything from *'printer near me'* to *'sushi near me'* or *'key cutter near me'*. For your Google My Business listing to be placed in the top three results for these kinds of searches, a series of continuous actions needs to be taken. This includes updating content regularly, adding keywords, service areas, categories and detailed business information to your listing. Certain components on your website pages and franchisee pages (microsites) can also dramatically increase the chances of your Google My Business listing appearing in the top three local search results. Those are also known as local SEO (Search Engine Optimisation) or local search marketing.

Google might sometimes automatically create a Google My Business listing for your franchise. It is important to claim ownership of that listing if it exists, otherwise some of your competitors might do. Not sure how to find out if you have a listing? Just go to Google and run a search of your company name and a location you have a franchisee at. Any business listing in the top right corner of the page with a map result, business details and so forth, means your company is in the directory. But if you see only website results on there, chances are that you are missing out on a great opportunity.

What makes Google My Business so powerful? First and foremost, it allows users to contact your franchise in various ways – to make a direct phone call or request driving directions to your location. In this way, it brings you footfall, drives website traffic and encourages people to go to the microsites of your franchisees. If you are a hotel or restaurant, customers can make reservations. But the best part is that you get monthly analytics of how many people have phoned you, asked for driving directions to your business or have visited your website from the listing. Those are genuine leads and are absolutely free. Read that again. It costs you nothing to be registered.

Once you have registered each of your franchise locations in Google's directory, you will notice the reviews section on there. As you know, there is an intrinsic relation between online reputation and lead conversion, and it is explicitly demonstrated in this aspect of Google My Business. If your franchise appears in the top three results under the map in a Google search and has zero reviews or an average score of two stars, while your competitors have five-star reputation, who do you think a client will contact?

CASE STUDY – MBE AUSTRALIA

A few years ago, I worked with the international franchise Mail Boxes Etc. in Australia. Their main activities are printing and courier services and virtual mailboxes. Back then, they numbered 23 locations across the country and had never included local marketing and Google My Business as part of their marketing strategy. Another challenge was that all of their listings in the directory were full of inconsistent information and the same was true all over the internet –

business working hours, addresses, phone numbers, and so forth were incorrect.

We deployed a comprehensive strategy for all 23 locations. We cleaned up the inconsistent information throughout the web, as well as populated Google My Business with updated business details, descriptions, photos and categories. After only three months these were the results:

- 21 out of 23 MBE Google My Business listings appeared on the top page of Google search results for '*printing services [area]*'.

- 22 out of 23 MBE Google My Business listings appeared on the top page of Google search results for '*courier [area]*'.

- 23 out of 23 listings appeared on the top page of Google search results for '*mailboxes [area]*'.

This led to an average 300% increase in traffic to the website from the listing, and 79% more phone calls and web enquiries. If you'd like to know more about how we did it exactly, download the full case study from our website on www.franchisefame.com/book.

CASE STUDY – MBE DOMINICAN REPUBLIC

Another great example of the power of local marketing is our more recent work with Mail Boxes Etc. in the Dominican Republic. When we initially started work on their local presence, some of the franchisees there didn't even have Google My Business, so we had to create and verify some. Others needed verification only, and one needed a total revamp. An additional challenge was the fact that they were all individual listings and had to be managed separately, whereas when you are a franchise or a multi-location business, Google allows you to have a 'location group' account, where you can manage all locations easily. And to make it even more challenging, because of the lack of postcodes in the Dominican Republic, the locations those listings were pointing to were not always correct, and because of that, it was almost impossible to verify those locations.

Again, after three months of continuous effort and liaising with Google support, we managed to create a joined account for all twenty franchisee listings. The franchisor could easily manage changes in the working hours and other business details. Populating the listings with fresh, brand-consistent content also dramatically improved their local placement in Google searches, as well as the number of phone calls and visits they received.

- Each centre had a 107% increase in calls received.
- 16 out of 20 franchise locations had their Google My Business listing appear in the top three searches for the keywords of their choice.
- Driving direction requests from the listing to the stores increased by an average of 180%.

To learn more, head to our website and download the full case study at www.franchisefame.com/book.

Pay-per-click advertising

Another great way to support your franchisees is to launch an advertising campaign through Google Ads or social media ads, whichever is proven to work best for your specific audience and sector. The beauty of these digital marketing channels is that they can either work for the good of the whole franchise network or be set so that they aid the specific franchisees who need a push at that time.

A paid advertising campaign works best in combination with other marketing channels. For example, if the product or service your franchise delivers is so innovative that there is still little demand for it, that demand has to be created. This is where you raise awareness about your brand and educate the audience about your product, which is usually done through social media and/or display advertising. This period is often referred to as learning/educating.

Once your audience knows about you, it may take a while until they need your services, but once they do, chances are that they will search for you online and not on social media where they first heard about you. This is why you need to have a solid presence in the page-one search results. The more times your brand appears on Google when your ideal buyer searches for you, the higher the chances of them contacting your franchise are. This period is called conversion.

Let's say you are looking for 'handyman in Islington'. If the results contain the same brand multiple times – for example, you see a Google Ad for one particular brand, then you scroll down the page and you see the same brand in the local results with their Google My Business listing, and further down their website appears in the organic search results – the likelihood of you clicking on and contacting that brand are three times higher than those only appearing once. This is why Google Ads are extremely effective in a combination with local marketing, website SEO, and so forth.

Another great benefit of Google Ads is the fact that you can specifically target locations you'd like your ads to appear in. This provides a great opportunity for the franchising sector, as you could support certain franchisees with local ads without launching a national advertising campaign. For example, you could launch a three-month Google Ads campaign for each new franchisee that you have just onboarded, to help them gain traction and get their first clients. Or you could launch a campaign for a franchisee you have already identified is not doing so well with sales. The level of flexibility with Google Ads allows you to target specific postcodes and exclude others or draw a radius around the franchisees' locations. You can also exclude certain searches and mark them as negative so that your ad does not appear for them. The level of customisation of the ads is profound.

Consider your costs

It is important to know, however, that national Google Ads campaigns are most cost-effective in the long run. My agency has tried and tested that multiple times, and has always found that launching a nationwide campaign including all your franchise locations requires less advertising spend than if you launch individual ads per each franchisee location. The total ad spend of individual campaigns will always be higher than having a single ad campaign encompassing all franchisee locations. What you choose to go with will depend on your business objectives – whether you want to boost sales for particular franchisees or for all of them.

The question of cost often arises when making such considerations. Some franchisors charge franchisees a monthly contribution fee towards a national advertising campaign. The argument for this is that it costs less than them individually launching campaigns themselves. Of course, in this case you need to have franchisees unanimously agreeing to contribute towards this initiative, which, as we all know, can sometimes be an impossible mission.

Once you have decided what type of advertising you'd go for, there are more decisions to be made, such as what ad copy you will use. It is vital to make sure your ad copy is compelling and makes users click on the ad. Upon clicking, where would the ad take them? Landing pages generally work best, as you can populate those with specific content, plus you can optimise them for conversions. You could also send visitors from the ads to existing pages of your website, if you believe these are good enough to convert them into enquiries. From experience, landing pages with specific conversion-optimised content yield better results than just sending visitors to a website with many pages, as they can get lost searching for information and end up leaving without contacting you.

Create a marketing calendar

Creating a marketing calendar for your franchisees with all the activities that they need to do to stay in line with the overall strategy and plan of the brand is another way to ensure continuous support as well as consistency across the franchise units. Carefully planned marketing initiatives executed throughout the entire network go a long way. Here's an example for how to implement one:

- Plan the activities you'd like your franchisees to engage with in the following quarter.

- Create the social media posts they need to publish on their accounts.

- Design the flyers, banners, posters, email newsletters, etc that they should use to contact existing customers and potential leads. All the marketing material should follow the strategy for the quarter.

- Combine the resources into a document/folder with a calendar outlining the activity that needs to be undertaken per day of the week and distribute it throughout the network.

- Monitor its implementation per channel and franchisee and incentivise the ones in the network who follow it meticulously.

You can be as creative as you like, but always remember that you, the franchisor, are in service to your network. Consider what would be most helpful for them as well as your bottom line. Your role is to nurture the relationship, support them through their entrepreneurial journey, ensure they have the right environment for their business to thrive, and to guide them through difficult times towards a common goal. The success of your franchisees is also your own success.

Summary

- You are only as good as the weakest franchisee in your network.

- You can support your network of franchisees by setting up a franchisee committee of top performers and having honest conversations with them about what can be improved.

- Set up clear KPIs that measure the performance of the franchisees on a regular basis, with minimum targets for franchisees to reach.

- Have a support process in place if a franchisee does not hit the minimum threshold.

- Your franchise marketing needs to do the best for the network. Use local marketing campaigns, Google My Business, pay-per-click advertising and a strategic marketing action plan to achieve this.

FIVE

Focused Team

The third F of the model is dedicated to the help you need to develop your brand and make it a success. By now, you should have already realised that you cannot do it all yourself and recruited some talent to support you through the journey. But if you haven't yet, I hope this chapter will at least get you to reconsider. Running an ordinary business by yourself is not impossible, especially if you do not have aspirations to grow it and want to keep it a lifestyle type of business that pays the bills. With franchising, the situation is quite different, as franchising is all about growth and expansion. Building a team of focused A-players around you is crucial to accomplish that.

You do not lack time but priorities

Do you often feel that there aren't enough hours in the day to finish all your work tasks? Do you put in long hours and a 60- to 70-hour working week is not unusual? Are you swamped with emails and tasks that have been waiting for days to be picked up? It is not uncommon for franchisors to feel this way and to be buried in tasks, emails and meeting requests. Every one of us at some point of our entrepreneurial journey has felt this way. We tend to feel that we know our business best – which is almost always true – and that only we can do the best job – which is almost always wrong.

If you tried to launch a Google Ads campaign, for example, all by yourself and you had never done that before, it would probably take you days, if not weeks. First you have to research how to set up an account, then create tracking on your website, build campaigns, write compelling ad copy, set up the correct targeting, sort out billing – and you can easily get lost halfway through. Even if you didn't, that does not guarantee you that the ad campaign will be successful. You'd end up throwing money down the drain. In the end, you would seek help, but having already wasted both time and money. A certified specialist, on the other hand, who has done hundreds of Google Ads campaigns could do a great job, not only better than you, but also much faster, and in this way, be more cost-effective and efficient.

I remember listening to the InDent business podcast episode, 'How to Shift from Functional to Vital', and there was something they said that resonated with me strongly.[4] The podcast discussed productivity and the fact that entrepreneurs often say that they do not have time. The thing that I heard that made a huge impact on me was the fact that often it isn't time that we lack, but priorities. If we prioritised better and delegated everything not on the high-priority list, our lives would be so much simpler, and time would not be such a scarce resource. I dwelled upon that for a while. It made perfect sense. We only lack time when we try to do it all ourselves. We fail to distinguish the tasks that must absolutely be done by us, and what can be delegated to the team around us.

Does this strike a chord? Running a business is already a demanding and time-consuming task. Managing a franchise, focusing on new business development, recruitment, finance, marketing, communications, and so forth, are all too much for one person, no matter how good you are.

Over the years working with different franchisors, I've seen a lot. In one case, the CEO of a global franchise brand did not want to spend too much on hiring a team for the head office and kept on hiring interns. Interns are great for certain tasks, but they lack the skill set and experience to steer a franchise in the right direction. They are great for delegating low-value activities to, predominantly admin work, so that they can get a taste of what your business is like and learn about its processes and its operations. They

---

4   G Carlson, Episode 20: InDent – 'How to Shift from Functional to Vital', Dent: The Podcast (31 August 2016), www.keypersonofinfluence.com/ep-20-the-inaugural-indent-how-to-shift-from-functional-to-vital, accessed 13 February 2022

should not be hired for senior roles, nor tasked with tackling the challenging, complex tasks that the success of your franchise relies on.

Another franchisor was unfortunate enough to think that he was the only one who could do a good job. He thought he did not need any marketing or operations managers for the head office and wanted to do it all by himself. His failure to prioritise and delegate tasks was his nemesis. As you can imagine, he did not make it far without some help. As much as he had the passion and drive, and, to some extent, the skill set to succeed and take his franchise to the next level, he couldn't cope with all the tasks – countless conversations with franchisees and vendors, managing recruitment and new business development, qualifying new leads who wanted to invest in his franchise, and so on. It was his misjudgement that cost him almost a year of trying to grow his franchise with not much success. At the time, he was working his hardest, investing many hours and still not succeeding. It was incredibly frustrating for him despite all his efforts.

There is one thing both these cases have in common. They were not focusing on the right aspects of their business. In other words, they were lacking priorities. That led to them feeling frustrated and unsuccessful, worried, and even sometimes lonely. Can you relate? Many of us have felt this way at some point of our entrepreneurial journey, whether this was when we faced failure or when we were grinding but not reaching the desired results. This can be demotivating and discouraging. Often the problem lies with something as simple as not setting the business priorities straight.

Yes, you need to focus on high-value tasks that are important for the business. But at the same time, there are other low-value tasks that still need to be taken care of so that the franchise operations run smoothly. You need the best help you can get to achieve the results you are aiming for. Not hiring a focused, ambitious and experienced team to have your back will cost you dearly in the long run. Rather than growing and expanding, you'll be stuck in the same spot. Surrounding yourself with a focused team of A-players is critical for the success of your franchise.

CASE STUDY – FANTASTIC SERVICES

This reminds me of the days when I was in charge of the marketing and branding divisions of *Fantastic Services*. The company was growing exponentially, and new teams and projects were being created at speed. Everyone was overworked and stretched to their maximum capacity. Apart from being accountable for all marketing and branding activities, I was transitioning from another role and still had a sales team under my direct supervision. I worked long hours and, for a while, tried to do it all by myself, which resulted in even longer hours, extra work over the weekend and unnecessary stress. I was on the verge of burnout and constantly felt helpless and unfulfilled.

One day when I least expected it, I got called to the CEO's office. *Now what?* I remember thinking. *Another project?*

Another task I have to take on? Thankfully, it was not that. The CEO had noticed my struggle. He thoughtfully suggested hiring my very own PA to help me with my low-value tasks and to delegate the functional activities to. He also coached me to appoint the right people as leaders of each team I was in charge of – something that changed the way we worked entirely, as I had to communicate ideas and tasks to a few more senior people rather than twenty at any given time.

My efficiency and productivity hit the charts. The changes had such a positive effect that in a couple of months, one of the teams and I received a prestigious internal award for breaking the company's all-time records.

Prioritising and delegating tasks

There really is no excuse for not having the best people by your side today. In the old days, things used to happen differently. There were limited resources and a narrow talent pool to choose from, all based around a small geographical area. Talent was scarce, specialists incredibly hard to find and they came at a high cost. But with the power of technology today, we are able to choose and recruit the best talent from all over the world, and at competitive rates too.

Working with distant teams is a reality now more than ever, especially in a post-pandemic world. Platforms like Fiverr, Freelancer.com and Upwork are thriving, where you can either outsource specific tasks or hire a part-time or full-time specialist to help you with the tasks that you know are important for the business and you cannot do yourself. A virtual CFO is another similar, incredibly popular service where for a few hours a week, you get access to the best financial planners and consultants to help you stay on top of your finances, build your profit and loss statements and forecast your finances. And you can do all of this without the burden of a payroll, whereas back in the day, this was not an option.

The value ladder

Another way of looking at prioritising and delegating tasks is from the perspective of the value ladder. Imagine all the tasks and projects your franchise has got pending at that moment. Each one has to be allocated a step on the ladder. At the top of the ladder are the high-value tasks and at the bottom the low-value ones. A high-value activity would be anything that is of great importance to the franchise – for example, its finances and growth strategy (royalties, new business development, etc). These are activities that you should focus your attention on and carefully strategise, plan, assign and monitor their execution. Low-value activities, on the other hand, would be things that are not essential for the existence of the franchise, but are still important for running the day-to-day activities, such as franchisee network communication, website updates, and other admin.

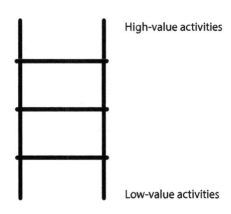

Visualising your priorities in this way allows you to focus your attention and time – which, by the way, is your most valuable resource – on the high-value tasks for the business. You should be spending time only on the activities that will have the highest impact, value or return on investment. Anything else, you can delegate to your team.

Vital versus functional tasks

Another model for delegating work is to separate the vital tasks from the functional ones. Vital tasks are those that make your franchise profitable, such as finding a new franchisee for a specific location or collecting royalties. Functional activities, on the other hand, keep the franchise running but are not essential for its existence and profitability. They are also known as operational tasks and can be prioritised second or delegated to a team member.

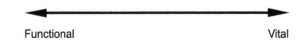

How much of your time at the moment is being spent on functional tasks? What is the percentage of time you spend on vital activities for the business? How many of the functional activities can you delegate to a team member so that you can free up more time for vital work?

Take a moment and use either of the two models to visualise what a day's work for you looks like. Position the activities that matter most for the profitability, strategy or expansion of your franchise on the highest steps of the ladder or on the right side of the axis, and the ones that are purely operational and admin-focused at the bottom of the ladder or the left end of the axis. At first, you might think that some activities are crucial for the business's success, but the more time you spend on the exercise, the clearer you will be that you could assign them to someone else from your team or even outsource them without having major impact.

In-house team or agency?

The challenge of finding help for your business is in recruiting a focused team and retaining it. There has always been an argument for and against hiring an agency to do some of the work versus creating an in-house team. There are many pros and cons behind both options. Let's explore some of them here.

Having an in-house team gives you more control and flexibility over their time and workload. Your in-house team will know the business best and will also adhere to all internal policies. You have their full and undivided attention and time. But this comes with the cost of adding more people to the payroll, which might be difficult and strenuous for a new franchise. Often franchisors seek one person who can do it all – a website specialist, plus a marketing guru, a great people person with comprehensive knowledge of the law, expertise in accounting, the list goes on. In business, these people are called unicorns. It is very hard to find a unicorn and even harder to pay them what they deserve.

Working with an agency, on the other hand, gives you access to an unlimited talent pool. For the price of one in-house person (or often even cheaper than having someone on a payroll), you get access to half a dozen vertically integrated specialists – a Google Ads expert, a designer, a web developer, a project manager, copywriter, and so forth. One drawback is that you get less focus on your business as their attention is split between a number of clients. But do not forget that a specialist might need thirty minutes to do something while someone inexperienced in-house may take hours or even days.

Some agencies design their products so that they can serve as your extended marketing arm, where you have full flexibility and access to their resources without the liability of them being on the payroll. There are agencies out there that will work with you on a monthly retainer and let you access their resources on an ad hoc basis, only using whatever you need from their talent pool. That could be consulting services one month, and full pay-per-click campaign management the other.

In my agency, we always adapt our approach to meet the needs of our customers. In some cases, we only do advisory consulting and auditing of the franchise's existing marketing team. In other cases, my team and I strategise and execute the whole marketing plan and activities on behalf of the franchisor, because they lack the resources to do so. Mixed models are the most common, where my team and I work under the guidance of a marketing manager and execute campaigns and support franchisees locally.

The bottom line is that both working with an agency or having an internal team could work for your franchise, and what you choose would probably depend on the size of your business. Franchises that are just starting out may not be able to afford to hire a great team right away and would need to start small. Working with an agency or a freelancer towards achieving growth and expansion would be the most suitable solution for them. Once the network of franchisees grows, the need for an operations and/or marketing manager arises. Then the franchise can afford to hire extra help, so potentially a mixed model of a small team and an agency would suit its needs.

How to choose the right agency

There is still a lot of negativity around working with agencies, sometimes because of previous poor experience, or because of the misconception that agencies charge more than hiring someone in-house. How do you choose a good agency to work with when there is so much noise out there and everyone seems to be banging on their chest that they are the best? Well, a few important considerations must be made.

First, make sure that the agency specialises in the sector that you are in, not just franchising but even more specifically the service sector, hospitality, beauty, care, etc. Second, make sure you ask for some case studies and references, so that you can speak to other franchisors whom the agency has worked with and know that they have a proven track record. Pay attention to how they approach your business. Do you feel that they understand its core values and your needs and objectives? Or do you feel that you are just another customer and you are getting templated answers, proposals and sales? Do you feel that they understand the problem they need to solve? Have they provided you with the best strategy, implementation plan and ways to track performance and success? Lastly, do they carefully define success with you and set clear and specific goals? Was return on investment discussed?

Your budget will also play an important role in your decision-making, of course, but it should not be your main criterion. Do not be fooled by major discounts where in the proposal 70% of the cost is slashed, and you now have a week to sign up for this one-off offer. Marketing and sales gimmicks like these try to create a sense of urgency in you to make a sale. A good agency methodically tries to understand your pain points: its team members ask the right questions and listen more than they speak. They then provide a custom solution to your problem that addresses your needs and objectives. Ideally, their proposal matches your budget too or they work with you to create a comprehensive plan adapted to your budget. Being candid and explaining what is feasible with what you can afford through setting milestones and deliverables for them is always a plus. The agency should ultimately feel like an extension of your own team.

Weighing up costs

One of the obvious objections to hiring help with your business is cost. Many franchisors fear that they cannot afford to hire more people or use someone external. While this may be true if you are just starting out and you are short on resources, once you have even a small network of franchisees, you are responsible for constantly demonstrating how the royalties you collect represent good value for money.

This means that a focused and well-qualified franchise management team is essential for the business. Apart from its internal support function, the team serves as the eyes and ears of the business and stays alert about any market changes, innovations and new competitors emerging. It guards the franchise against complacency and makes sure it keeps a competitive edge. But if the franchisees feel that the management service fees/royalties are not being used to the best of the network, the opposite can happen. They start considering exiting the business or acting outside the prescribed boundaries of their role.

Cost is always a valid objection. But speaking from experience, not growing your franchise and missing opportunities will cost you a lot more in the long term than hiring a focused team. Think about it like this – how much would it cost you if you decided to do it all by yourself and you made a mistake?

Let's say you decide to hold off on hiring a marketing agency to generate franchise recruitment leads and to support your existing franchisees with client leads. You try to do it yourself. You launch two separate campaigns on Facebook and Google Ads, each costing £1000 per month. It takes a couple of months for you to realise and admit that the campaigns are not successful. You have already wasted at least five hours a week of your valuable time. Plus, you have ended up having a franchisee throw in the towel as there was no new business coming in. On top of all that, you have not sold a single franchise unit for those two months and you have spent a minimum of £2000, plus forty hours of your time. If we modestly estimate your time at a rate of £25 per hour, this adds another £1000 to the cost of the experiment. This mistake has cost you £3000, not to mention the lost opportunity of selling one or more franchise units.

Does looking at it in this way put things in perspective? Hiring someone to do the job for you would have cost a fraction of this, and would have provided a return on investment through new franchise sales and royalties from franchisee revenue. There are specialists out there that are much better in their field of work than you. Seek and hire talent like that, and try to ignite in them the same passion you hold for your business.

Summary

- Setting the right priorities will free up a lot more time for you to focus on the business.

- Use visualisation tools to prioritise high-value, vital activities and delegate or outsource low-value, functional tasks.

- Surrounding yourself with A-players is crucial for success.

- Not delegating tasks to your team members could cost you dearly.

- An agency can serve as your extended focused team.

- The cost of performing a task yourself and making a mistake could be much higher than hiring someone to do the job for you.

SIX

Full Funnel

The fourth F is all about keeping your funnel full with high-quality, relevant leads. Franchise growth is based entirely on selling new territories and in this way achieving expansion, while collecting franchise fees (royalties) from the existing franchisee network. The franchise model relies heavily on these two main revenue streams. Growth is at the root of franchising, and this is great as it promotes continuous development and improvement. Anyone who is not ready to scale up and develop further is probably not a good fit for any franchise.

Looking back to how things were done before the age of digital marketing, it was all much more complicated. Selling your franchise and generating leads were only happening around franchising events, exhibitions, expos, and advertising in offline media, such as magazines, journals and directories. This came at a high cost and was extremely time-consuming. Not every franchisor could afford to exhibit their business at a franchise fair, for example. Today it is easier and more cost-effective to reach a wider audience with the power of digital marketing and technology. It all starts, however, with knowing who you are after.

Buyer personas

Many franchisors, often those who are new to the job, make one fatal mistake that dooms their hard work to failure. They think they can sell their franchise to nearly anyone. They are so focused on thinking 'no experience is needed' or 'anyone can do it' that they sabotage their own business growth at the earliest stage.

In franchising, there is a common misconception that if you have done it yourself – built a brand from zero, made it a successful business, dealt with all the paperwork and legalities around franchising it out – then anyone can do it. It may be true to some extent that the business should be scalable and easy to replicate in another location, and that the skills you need to run it should be transferable from one person to another. But that does not mean that anyone can do it. Imagine shooting in the dark and hoping to hit a target. It is much the same when a franchisor is trying to sell their business idea to nearly everyone. Not every book is for every reader. Similarly, your franchise is not suitable for everyone who wants to run one.

Before launching any campaigns for lead generation purposes or spending any money on marketing, it is crucial to make sure you know who your ideal franchisee is. You need to be detailed when describing your ideal franchisee. This is your buyer persona, or customer avatar. Get into the nitty gritty, such as where they live, what their experience is, what background and demographic they come from, what education they have, and so on. Imagine you are in your ideal franchisee's shoes. What is their name? How old are they? Do they have any kids? What are their pains and problems? What are their best qualities? What drives them and what puts them off doing something? Spending time thinking about this is of great importance to the success of your lead generation campaigns. When you take a deep dive into your ideal franchisee's ambitions, fears, pains and problems, you will understand them fully and know how to package your proposition so that they buy into your business.

WANT TO KNOW MORE?

Head to www.franchisefame.com/book to download your free buyer persona template document. You can fill this in a few times to create at least three franchisee avatars. This exercise will deepen your understanding of who your ideal franchisee is, and will be extremely useful for your marketing team when targeting your campaigns later on.

CASE STUDY – BUYER PERSONAS IN PRACTICE

A couple of years ago, we had a franchisor contact the agency asking for help with their lead generation. He and his team had created a great website with comprehensive information about the franchise opportunity, and had a proven track record of business success and a couple of successful franchisees. They were spending a decent amount of money on ads but somehow were not achieving the right results. The leads were scarce, and their quality was not great either. They couldn't believe there were so few people who would want to buy into this otherwise great business.

After discussing their objectives, and analysing and auditing all the results – tracking metrics, landing pages, and campaigns – we established that the audience of the ads was extremely broad. The franchisor was spending most of his budget to reach people who were not relevant and would not be interested in buying a franchise. We sat with the franchisor and brainstormed who exactly their ideal franchisee was. We created a few buyer personas and then applied them to narrow down the audience of the ads.

Within a few weeks, conversions went up dramatically. Not only that, but the campaigns became more cost-effective and the cost per lead was lower, which meant that ultimately for the same budget, the franchisor was getting a lot more value and leads. Soon enough, he made his first franchise sale, which provided a great return on investment and advertising budget for the next few months. Something as small as defining your audience makes such a huge impact.

The marketing funnel

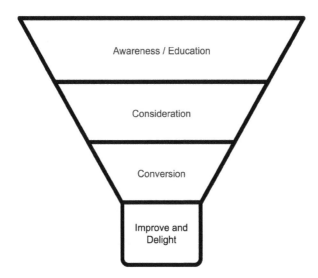

There are various interpretations of the marketing funnel model, but most commonly, it illustrates the stages a user goes through when engaging with a brand and its products. Those are:

- Awareness (also referred to as education)
- Consideration
- Conversion
- Improve and delight

In the awareness stage, the brand educates its audience about its products, presenting the opportunity and the solution to an already identified problem. The user then enters the consideration stage, which could last from a couple of minutes to a couple of months, or sometimes even years, depending on the value and cost of the product and whether it prompts a spontaneous buying decision or something that requires planning and research. The conversion stage usually takes place on the brand's own media, such as its website, social media page, online shop, etc, and it is the stage where the user either purchases the product or shows interest in buying through making an enquiry. Last but not least, the improve and delight stage focuses on improving the overall buying experience to increase conversions, retain customers and encourage repeat sales.

Each stage works in tandem to create a path for your buyer, through which they engage with your franchise before making a purchase decision. It is important that you understand the stages so that you can design the buying journey to influence the audience and capture their interest (and investment) at the end of it.

Let's look at some of the ways you can take the buyer through the funnel from education to conversion and, ultimately, delight.

Landing pages

Once you are certain whom exactly you are after, the next step is to make sure that you give them a crystal-clear idea about the opportunity you are offering them. You should describe this on a beautifully designed franchise brochure and a landing page where you are directing your leads to. Think about all the questions a potential franchisee might ask you, such as the initial investment required, when they are expected to break even, the support they'll get, the training they'll undertake, the amount of royalty fees they'll need to pay, etc. You need to present all this information in a concise and clear way. If you do not feel comfortable sharing the exact investment or operating capital needed to start the franchise, you do not have to, but you need to then be even more specific with the rest of the information you give so that you can attract visitors to send an enquiry.

Naturally, the landing page has to be designed to lead the user to a particular action, whether that's to download a brochure and leave their contact information, or call you and ask about the opportunity. This is probably the most important step from the lead generation process. Over the years, I have seen many good-looking web pages that received high amounts of traffic from ads, but which simply did not convert into enquiries. Having a clear call to action message is a priority.

A common mistake people make here is stuffing the pages with too many elements and call to action messages, such as where a user can download a brochure, make an enquiry, go through a quiz of questions, phone you and submit an application online. All these options are overwhelming, and the visitor is much more likely to leave the page without contacting you at all. Instead, drive the user to complete one simple action.

Other elements of a great landing page optimised for conversions are interviews and testimonials from existing franchisees. There is nothing more reassuring for your leads to see that they will be surrounded by a group of successful peers. Showcasing your awards and accreditations is another great way to demonstrate your credibility and authority. Any recognitions from other organisations or industry governing bodies are a trust factor and will put the readers at ease while they familiarise themselves with your franchise. Lead magnets such as downloadable case studies and additional information about the investment and capital can be neatly organised in a PDF document, which can be made available for download on the page in exchange for some personal details. This offers a perfect way to capture the data of potentially interested prospects, who you can contact later and have a conversation with.

A Q&A section is always a great idea too. Make sure you include answers to questions such as how long the qualification process would take, or what marketing support you provide to new franchisees as part of their training and onboarding package. Use captured personal data for email marketing, where you introduce the opportunity in more detail. The decision to invest in a business and buy a franchise is not an impulsive one and it often takes time for people to think the idea over before they make an initial contact.

WANT TO KNOW MORE?

Download our guide, The Anatomy of a Landing Page, from our website: www.franchisefame.com/book.

Lead generation campaigns

After you have secured a conversion-optimised landing page, the next step is to plan, build and launch your campaign. Depending on your buyer persona, you can use different marketing channels, including Facebook, LinkedIn, Google, etc. This is where the magic happens and where most franchisors need specialist advice and help.

Regardless of the channel you pick, building a lead generation campaign can be a difficult and sometimes almost impossible job, unless you are a seasoned marketer with at least a few years of experience. I highly recommend seeking professional help for this step of the process, whether you hire a freelance ads specialist or outsource it to an agency. At this point it gets slightly too technical and analytical to do on your own. You will need a designer to create beautiful visuals for any display materials, a technical pay-per-click specialist to build optimised and cost-effective campaigns, as well as some development work to help you install tracking tools on your landing page.

My agency is often hired to help with recruitment lead generation for franchises that either people have never heard of or did not even know were businesses that can be franchise-able. As with the marketing funnel, we first educate the audience about the opportunity. This usually takes place on platforms such as social media, YouTube or third-party websites, where the audience can see short videos or animated banner ads about the franchise opportunity. The idea is then planted in their head. They may

91

or may not have looked into it and visited your website to learn more. In the next few days and even weeks, the ads follow them on other websites and platforms and carefully and subtly remind them about the opportunity (remarketing). The more times your audience sees your brand and interacts with it, even subconsciously, the better.

Because a decision to quit a nine-to-five job and invest in a new business is not a light-hearted decision to make, it often takes them weeks to come into contact with your brand and submit an enquiry. But when they do, they usually go on Google and search for a *'franchise opportunity'* or something even more specific such as *'buy a franchise in [area]'*. This is why it is ideal if they have come across your brand at least five times already, so that the chances of them searching for *'[your brand name] franchising opportunities'* dramatically increases. This stage is the conversion stage. Once they have found your landing page with the opportunity and have read through it in more detail, ideally, they should leave their information and request a call or download a brochure. The lead is now real and it should either hit your inbox or drop into a CRM system if you use one.

Tracking tools

To measure the success of the campaigns, you need to have the right tracking systems installed on your landing page or website. I am personally adamant about tracking because this is how the return on investment from any campaign or marketing initiative is measured. Anything else is just guestimates. This step gets techy, and if you do not come from a marketing or programming background, it can be a little complicated. Tracking tools such as Google Analytics, Google Tag Manager, Facebook and LinkedIn pixels, heatmaps, and other session recording tools analyse the performance of your digital marketing campaigns. By setting specific goals and pre-defined criteria in Google Analytics, you can receive information like the number of visitors that landed on your pages, the actions they took, where they dropped off, and so on.

Good metrics to keep an eye on are conversion rate per channel, cost per lead per channel, cost per acquisition per channel, and so on. You can track each stage of the marketing funnel till the very end, so you can also determine the quality of the leads per channel. All of this, of course, is relevant if you are running more than one campaign across various channels such as Facebook, LinkedIn, Google, franchising directories, etc.

Let's imagine you're spending £1000 on a Facebook advertising campaign, another £1000 on Google Ads and another £1000 on LinkedIn. If you don't know where your leads are coming from, how would you know which one of the three is the most successful campaign and which provides the best return on investment? How would you calculate the cost per lead or cost per acquisition from each of the channels so that you understand which one is the most cost-effective and top performing at the same time? On the flip side, what if you knew that Facebook generated ten leads, LinkedIn five and Google twenty for the same amount spent. It is much easier to decide to ramp up the channel bringing most leads at the lowest cost per lead, isn't it? This is how important tracking and measuring success of a campaign is.

Conversion tracking plays a pivotal role in the last stage of the marketing funnel, improve and delight. This is where your marketing team carefully analyses the results and improves the campaigns so that they become more efficient and effective and bring an even higher ROI. This stage involves the use of the tracking systems you should have already put in place.

The data compiled after at least a month of running the ads should be sufficient for analysis. If the campaigns were initially built to test different ad variations, the idea here is to check how the change in ad copy, visuals and other parameters influenced the results. This is also the stage where you can make small alterations to the landing page to improve conversions. In digital marketing, this process is referred to as conversion rate optimisation or CRO, and it usually requires the skill set and expertise of a team, rather than a single person.

The delight part comes from the fact that you create campaigns that the users are delighted by, that answer their exact needs and solve their problems, so that for them, deciding to engage with your franchise really is a no-brainer.

CASE STUDY – CENTRAL AMERICA

Not long ago, we were contacted by a franchisor from Central America. Their main challenge was franchise recruitment lead generation. The number of leads that they received was not high enough, the quality of the leads was not ideal and the cost per conversion from their campaigns was too high. Another challenge was the fact that the brand was not recognisable in the countries of target, namely Costa Rica and Panama. To make it worse, their franchise opportunities website wasn't performing ideally either.

We stepped in with a comprehensive strategy. We revised their target audience and created a clear buyer persona. Next, based on the challenges and their strategic objectives, we launched two types of campaigns with different purposes – one for raising brand awareness (education) and another one to attract enquiries (conversion). We created a beautifully designed and clear landing page, where the leads were sent to leave their contact details and request a call back.

The campaign duration was eight months, during which our primary aim was to improve conversions and optimise the efficiency of the ads (improve and delight stage).

As a result, we managed to achieve the following:

- The number of leads increased from 14 to 149 per month as a direct result of our work. That is an astonishing 964%.

- Because of the continuous optimisation of the campaigns and improvements made on the landing pages, the cost per conversion decreased by a whopping 83%. That meant more value for the advertising budget of the franchisor.

The franchisor was extremely happy with our help and this was the beginning of a fruitful collaboration.

All of this work can sound a bit overwhelming and complicated. It really shouldn't be if you have the right resources and help to guide you through the process. Over the years, I've heard all sorts of excuses, such as lead generation being too expensive, too difficult, impossible to track or too complicated. Nothing in business is expensive if it generates a return on investment. Spending a couple of thousand pounds on lead generation might sound like a lot, but what if that brought you twenty qualified leads of potential franchise buyers? Would that still be expensive? And what if out of those twenty leads you managed to reach an agreement with two potential partners? This same campaign already gives a great return on investment and pays off your marketing and advertising budget for the next six months.

Alternatively, you could make the mistake of trying to do it all by yourself and fail, or sit and wait for potential buyers to find you themselves, which will only increase the chance of you feeling unaccomplished and frustrated for months and months, of you losing opportunities and time while you focus on low-value activities and wonder why your business is not working despite your best efforts. Meanwhile, your competitors will be selling and opening franchises in the areas where you wanted to step in and will be getting a bigger market share.

A much better image is the one of you focusing on franchise sales and lead qualification, growing your business, selling new territories you didn't even dream of, and feeling successful and fulfilled, while generating a great return on investment and having a franchise marketing partner that you can rely on by your side. Which of the two routes you decide to pursue is entirely up to you.

Summary

- Keep your funnel always full with high-quality leads.

- Use a detailed buyer persona to target your lead generation campaigns.

- Optimise your landing pages for conversions by giving detailed information about the franchise opportunity.

- Build cost-effective campaigns and outsource this where appropriate.

- Constantly look to optimise and improve results.

- Analyse and measure ROI so you can do more of what works.

SEVEN

Finding The Fit

The fifth and last F is all about finding the right fit for your franchise. What if I told you that less is more and actually fewer franchise sales are better than more? You would think that is counterintuitive, right? With the risk of repeating myself, I will say it again – not every book is for every reader. Sometimes it is better to withhold a sale rather than sell your business concept to anyone for the sake of generating revenue. This chapter looks at the best ways to handle a franchise lead once it has hit your CRM system.

Less is more

While many franchisors fall into the trap of thinking that their business is suitable for nearly everyone, others are inclined to compromise their success by selecting franchisees who do not fully meet the criteria. Franchisors do this to get franchise fee income and recover the investments they've made in recruitment, legal advice, marketing, and so forth. This usually causes regret on both sides.

Underestimating all the hard work you have invested to create this business and franchise it out is very common in the sector, as is underestimating the skill set required to run a unit as a franchisee. Trust me when I say this, that does not mean you should not have any minimum requirements. Your franchise is not suitable for everybody, and that is fine. It only means that you need to carefully select from the pile of applications you should have if you followed the advice in the previous chapter. And to be able to select the right candidates, you need a solid lead qualification process.

CRM and lead qualification

Once you have generated the leads to fill your funnel, your lead qualification process should help you filter those leads to focus on the prospects who have the most potential. After all, selecting your partner is like a marriage – you want to make sure that you have the perfect partner with whom to embark on this business venture. Finding the perfect fit for the position might seem like a difficult task, but if the right structure is in place, it will be straightforward.

The successful franchisors I worked with over the years all had a solid step-by-step lead qualification process from the moment the lead showed interest and hit their CRM system. If your business does not currently use a CRM system for your franchise leads, I strongly recommend you change that as soon as possible. Any free one would do the job, but you need to make sure that your landing pages, all campaigns that are running, all advertising, marketing and even third-party portals are connected with it. In this way, once someone takes interest in your franchise, the lead hits the system and all their details are recorded, as well as where they came from. This goes hand in hand with the section in the previous chapter, 'Tracking tools'.

Why is having a CRM system in place that important? Well, first because of process automation. There are certain campaigns and marketing initiatives that you can auto-mate through the system – for example, the initial email a lead receives after registering interest in your franchise. Another benefit is the fact that you will have all your leads in one place, where you can easily manage them. You can run group email or text message campaigns, analyse sales and marketing data, measure the success of your marketing efforts, and calculate return on investment. Last but not least, a CRM system allows you to keep track of the progress each lead is making through the lead qualification process you have designed for them, while avoiding mistakes, repe-tition or omitting any important steps in this process.

Email drip campaigns

Once a lead hits your email and/or CRM system, it is common practice in the industry to confirm receipt of their message with an automated response. That response can be part of a whole email campaign, which is first triggered by an action such as someone filling out a form on your website and registering their interest. This automated email campaign is also known as a drip campaign in marketing terms, and usually works the following way. A lead receives an email right away, and then more are sent out to them at an interval of a few days up to a few weeks.

This is a great way to inform the lead about the process they are about to go through, telling them what to expect. It also provides the opportunity to educate them further about the opportunity, your brand, the team behind it, your story, values, and so on. Keeping an open 'dialogue' with the franchisee candidate keeps the lead warm, so that when you decide to contact them for a call or a meeting, they know exactly who you are.

Consider the possibility that they are shopping around and contacting multiple franchisors, as they have not decided which franchise they would like to invest in. Small things like the way you handle their enquiry and how you communicate with your franchisee candidates can either make or break the relationship.

Text message campaigns

Text message campaigns are another popular way to stay in touch with your franchise leads. Sending them a text with a link to an application form, or just reminding them where they are in the process and what to expect next can be a powerful way to keep the lead warm and engaged. This is especially true if the text message campaigns are planned in accordance with the email campaigns you are sending out. You can also minimise no-shows at meetings and calls when you send a text reminder an hour prior to the meeting, for example. Text message campaigns can be used to collect feedback after a meeting, too, to ask questions, or to warm up leads for the next stage of the process.

Another benefit of text message campaigns, much like email marketing, is their incredibly low cost. There are many online tools out there providing text message packages at a cost as low as 0.03 pence per text. Others have gone one step further and have integrated their text messaging functionality in their CRM software. A handful of software providers give you the option to design and send email campaigns and text messages to your database of leads.

But beware. Texting can be overkill if not done right or overused. Your message campaign could backfire and your company be perceived the wrong way. Remember to ask yourself if you'd like it if someone texted or emailed you every day. You do not want to put off a lead because you have been too insistent and have sent them dozens of texts that they did not respond to.

Marketing collateral

This is the place to mention the importance of designing beautiful and informative brochures, leaflets, and presentations. When you are speaking to a potential business partner of yours in person, you will probably be sharing your vision for the future and where you'd like your franchise to go in the next few years. You may also find yourself sharing the problems you are solving and the mission you have taken on. This is all great, but it can be very conceptual. The physical incarnation of all of this is your marketing collateral. The brochure you design to present each candidate with is the tangible representation of what you are bringing to the table for this potential partnership.

This is the first physical touchpoint the candidate has with your business. By now, they may well have seen your landing pages, but they have not touched anything yet. The marketing collateral's design and finish therefore play an important role in the process. Make sure that the look and feel of the marketing materials is high-end and you take pride in distributing them. Get professional help with designing and wording the content, and make sure that the printing agency you are using understand the requirements around how the final product should look and feel.

The lead qualification process

The next step should be contacting the lead. You can either do this yourself or have another team member phone them for an initial introduction (or schedule an introductory call for a more convenient time). It is up to you to decide how much information you will disclose on that first call and whether a non-disclosure agreement is required. In your introduction, it is a great idea to share any materials about the opportunity with them, such as brochures, case studies, existing franchisee testimonials, etc. The first call also offers a fantastic opportunity for you to understand more about the candidate – their previous experience, aspirations, and motives behind wanting to buy a franchise. This is the time when you both learn about each other and check if there is any chemistry between you. Some franchisors even go the extra mile and include psychometric testing in the qualification process to better understand the character and behavioural traits of the candidate.

After the first call, you'll have probably formed an opinion. If they've ticked some of the boxes for the qualities and experience you'd like a future franchisee of yours to possess, you should move their application to the next stage for further screening. This either happens face-to-face or over a video call. Since they have made it this far, this generally means that you already have a good idea of whether you'd like this candidate to become your franchisee and you should be comfortable with sharing more information on the numbers and the nitty gritty of your business. Tempting as it may be to present your franchise in the best possible way, you need to try and stay as objective as possible. The candidate should be able to make a fully informed decision without hearing misleading and exaggerated claims.

It is probably a good time to introduce them to the ops manager or CEO, whoever is qualifying the leads, if that is not you. If you feel that you are disclosing any sensitive information, it is OK to ask the candidate to sign a non-disclosure agreement prior to the meeting. If you'd like them to provide any evidence of past experience, recommendations and referrals or other documents, this is the stage where you could try and obtain these, either prior to or after the meeting.

Open days

A great practice to introduce a franchise candidate to the way business is done, and for both of you to see if they are the right fit, is to have an 'open day', where franchisee applicants visit existing franchise locations. This gives them a deep dive into your franchise and places them in a real scenario environment. They meet with existing franchisees, gather experience first-hand and ask specific questions about the business ops. This experience is especially beneficial for the candidate, as it clears any doubts or uncertainties as to whether they would like to invest in your franchise and gives them the confidence that this is something they'd like to take on. Open days also provide a good opportunity for your top-performing franchisees to receive appreciation from the fact that their franchises are being used as an example and their expertise is valued.

From here on, the process depends on you. You can throw in as many other live or online meetings as you like if further professional vetting is required, or you can move straight to planning. This will involve drawing up a timeline, issuing the Franchise Information Memorandum (FIM), reviewing the franchise agreement, the candidate's business plan and financial projections, and so on.

At this stage, franchisors usually like to receive a deposit or initial payment of the franchise fee from the candidate. The first instalment can be anything from 10% to 40% depending on the overall investment. If the candidate is applying for a business loan to fund this, you might need to get involved in the application process. Once any financing is approved, the legal agreement is signed, and the rest of the fee should be transferred to you (ideally no later than five days prior to the commencement of the training). Then it is official – you have closed the deal and have another partner joining your franchise network.

Onboarding and training

To guarantee your new franchisee a successful start, a comprehensive training programme should be put in place. This should give them in-depth understanding of the franchise's business values, operations and company culture. In other words, you need to get them as excited about your franchise as you are. Passing on all the knowledge that you have about the industry, your business, sales, operations, marketing and recruitment is part of your role as a franchisor. This is what they buy into. Your experience, expertise and continuous support, and a carefully tailored training programme is all part of the franchise package.

Successful franchisors have a solid training programme for new recruits, but also provide ongoing training for their existing franchisees, because they understand the importance of continuous learning and improvement. Nothing in business remains the same – changes in the industry, updates to knowledge base, new emerging markets and increases in competition require ongoing training support to ensure you stay on top of your competitors and do not lose market share. With time, franchisee motivation may wane, certain skills need refreshing or further development is required. Training should be an ongoing theme and be enrooted in the culture of your franchise, not just part of the onboarding process.

There are companies out there that offer off-the-shelf training programmes and others that help you build a custom programme for your franchise. Whichever you choose, make sure that you design your training with the end customer in mind. How do you train the franchisees so that they deliver the best service at the highest level of quality? Break the training down into modules such as finance, operations, marketing, etc. Training should ideally be done in a special facility set up for this purpose, followed by a more hands-on experience at a franchisee's location.

It is also a good idea to involve some of your existing top-performing franchisees in the training process. You can incentivise them in different ways, but it is always best to have a few different trainers, some being peers, and others external to the organisation, as it makes training more comprehensive.

CASE STUDY – OVEN CLEANING

I still remember clearly my days as an oven cleaning franchisee. We would receive the occasional complaint from a customer, some of them because the technician seemed grumpy and did not smile or greet a client properly. And despite doing a great job, something that small impacted the overall quality of the service.

Training my team regularly and adopting new practices based on client feedback was essential for our success as a business. The training we received from head office seemed like common sense, but the lessons were valuable. We are all human, and as such we experience emotions and go through things. Everyone has a bad day sometimes – you can't control that. At training days, we would spend a lot of time on introductions, greetings, inspections at the end of a service, leaving marketing collateral at the client's property and even how to do upsells and cross-sells. These things seem simple but still need to be included in training and organised in an easy-to-remember, step-by-step process to minimise mistakes and complaints.

Today I still firmly believe that it is because of the initial onboarding and ongoing training courses we received from head office, alongside the internal training we organised for our oven cleaning technicians, that we had such great success and a high number of return customers.

Think differently about selling your franchise

If some of you are still in doubt as to why the lead quali-fication process and training programmes are needed, let's imagine the scenario where you sell the franchise to whoever wants to buy in and you do not provide them with any training whatsoever, because you think it is very simple and easy to grasp. Perhaps the service and business is technically easy to grasp, but franchisees should understand the specific operational practices of the business, be aware of its values and quality standards, learn about invoicing, the supply chain, and so much more. Picking the wrong partner can cost you not only your reputation along the line, but also months of hard work. Closing a franchise location or trying to resell it is much harder when a franchisee has already failed there. Then there's the struggle before the franchisee decides to exit the business – the numerous customer complaints, the unhappy franchisee spreading toxic behaviour throughout the network. The worst part is that you feel that you are not making any progress as a franchisor despite all your efforts.

As such, franchisors must not really sell franchises. This is a much-needed shift in thinking. The real role of the franchisor is to grant the business rights to qualifying candidates. You are entrusting your brand, system and know-how to another party, so it follows that you must exercise great care in choosing the right person to represent your business. The franchisee recruitment process is a two-way exercise. You need to interrogate candidates and be clear about their skills, motivation, experience, personal circumstances, financial position, etc.

There will be certain franchisees who perform better than others, and inevitably there will be some who do not do as well as you hoped. The lead qualification process is there to minimise that risk. The extensive training and development programmes serve to mitigate that risk too. It is your duty as a franchisor to create a nurturing environment of learning and support for your franchisees, so that when they come across a challenge, they will be able to overcome it with your help.

Imagine a future where you have managed expectations correctly from the start and picked the right candidate. You have added yet another valuable partnership to your business. Your franchisee network has expanded, and you now have a strong group of peers who will support you through your journey of growing the brand. The franchisees are happy and thriving, their revenue is growing, and so is yours. You have a steady lead flow of potential franchise buyers who would love to sample some of the success your existing network is reaping. How great would that be?

But this can only be achieved if you have followed the process and have found the right fit in your business partners. No exceptions. This will make sure that you surround yourself with emotionally invested partners who understand your mission and live the company values, and will guarantee your success through business growth and expansion.

Summary

- A lead qualification process is a must-have.

- How you design it is up to you, but always have the franchisee candidate in mind.

- Provide objective information without making misleading or exaggerated claims.

- Onboarding training programmes ensure you give a great head start to your newest partners.

- Involve top-performing franchisees in the onboarding and ongoing training processes.

- Regular training for your existing franchise network ensures you keep your competitive edge.

- Do not try to sell your franchise, but instead carefully select candidates to whom you will entrust the right to operate under your brand.

PART THREE

IMPLEMENTATION AND SCALING UP

Now you've been through each of the Five Fs, you have gained a deeper understanding of how all participating parties in franchising come together to achieve sustainable growth and soaring success. You have identified the gaps in your current marketing strategy and used the supporting materials and downloadable files to come up with a comprehensive action plan for implementing the Five Fs in your business.

In Part Three, we will be discussing the implementation of the model and some considerations if you are applying it on a global scale.

PART THREE

IMPLEMENTATION AND SCALING UP

EIGHT

Sustainable Growth And Success

You have now learned what the Five Fs of franchise marketing model consists of, and you have a deeper understanding as to how your fantastic reputation, franchisee network, focused team, full funnel, and finding the fit come into play when setting out to achieve your business objectives. Acknowledging each individual F is important, and understanding exactly what it comprises of and what parts of the business it concerns is essential. But the way that all of the five Fs come together is what makes the model so powerful.

The Five Fs work together

My team and I have tested the method numerous times. If implemented correctly, the model works without failure.

If you're at the beginning of your franchising journey and looking for your first pilot franchisee, that's great! You have not yet made the mistakes that would have cost you time and money, and you have the opportunity to get it right first time. If you are a franchisor with a number of retail units and franchisees, that's also great, because you have some serious experience and learning that you have gained over the years, and you can easily spot the positive effect the model will have on your franchise. Whether you've been in business for five or ten years, or only a couple, that does not matter. Nor does the nature of your business. The model is universal. It is applicable to any franchise that has the ambition and aspiration to grow through selling new territories while maintaining high franchisee satisfaction and success rates.

While reading the previous parts of the book, you might have had the feeling that some of the Fs overlap or cover similar sections of the business. You were absolutely right. This is because all five elements of the model are intrinsically connected, and together, they form a powerful bond that puts your franchise in position to achieve more ambitious goals than you have ever considered. Ignoring or removing one of the Five Fs would disrupt the balance of the model, and while you may still achieve some short-term results, sooner or later, your business would begin to falter.

Let's imagine you decide to only focus on expansion. You set specific targets – numbers of franchisees you'd like to sign, territories you'd like to sell into. You start aggressively focusing all your resources in that direction. Your time and marketing budget are dedicated to generating leads – as is your head office team. They work diligently with an agency that brings in the new recruits, and you and your team qualify, close deals and work on onboarding them.

Your existing franchisees are left unattended. A few of them express their dissatisfaction with the fact that there has been no marketing guidance from the top level. Others complain that their sales have plummeted and are unsure what local marketing initiatives they should be focusing on. Time passes and more franchisees start complaining, raising questions about what their marketing contribution is being used for. One or two of them express even stronger opinions and start considering an exit plan. You get a phone call one day, where they tell you that they have decided to leave, asking you to help them resell the franchise. While you were busy signing up new franchisees and trying to expand, you neglected your franchisee network and ended up losing two locations instead.

We can all agree that such a situation is far from ideal. Unfortunately, I have come across this scenario in franchising too often. If you follow the advice in this book, you will avoid making the same mistake.

The bottom line is that all five elements of the franchise marketing model are there for a reason, and none should be overlooked or underestimated. If you feel that you are doing particularly well with one of the Fs and are tempted to skim over it, go back to the chapter about it and look closely for ideas you might have missed out on. The model only works when all its components are applied as a whole.

Implementation – where to start

OK, you're on board and would like to start applying the model to your franchise right away. You are probably wondering where to begin. Don't fret if you notice the order of The Five Fs is different from the order I cover them in the chapters; for this exercise it's helpful to start by looking at your team. Let's get going!

Focused team

As a first step, it is a good idea to review your current team of head office employees. You will probably need specialist help for 'full funnel' and 'franchisee network', so consider hiring a marketing person and/or an agency to outsource some of the work to. If your network of franchisees is already well developed, you may also need an operations manager to help you with the daily ops of running a franchise.

Use the list of tasks you have created from the previous chapters and think about which ones you can delegate to team members. In your short- and mid-term planning, consider recruitment too. If you manage to sign another five new franchisees in the next quarter or year, how would this influence your head office team? Will you need to hire someone to support them, or can the current structure take on another five, ten or twenty new franchisees?

Franchisee network

Analyse the condition of your franchisee network by performing reviews and conducting group meetings with your franchisees. Identify top performers and low performers. Listen to franchisee feedback and try to understand where they need most support from you – local marketing, training and development, or perhaps staff recruitment?

Once you have identified the common themes, plan campaigns and procure resources to help them. Is the marketing budget sufficient, or are you going to need franchisees to contribute more locally? It is probably best to refer them to an approved provider they can use for local marketing, so that you can stay on top of all the initiatives and guarantee yourself brand consistency throughout the network, rather than them venturing out on their own.

Think about adding value for your network through negotiating great deals with vendors in your supply chain. Many agencies will agree to give you a more competitive rate for marketing services if you have all your franchisees participate, rather than if one approaches an agency individually. Other vendors will also negotiate good deals with you based on the volume of your network. Use it to your benefit.

Make meetings, conference calls and interviews a regular bi-monthly or quarterly practice, or arrange annual events for all franchisees, such as a conference. Appoint a franchise committee whose members will represent and defend the interests of all franchisees when making decisions concerning the whole network. Once you set up meetings and conference calls, adhere to those and do not miss or reschedule them. It is important for your franchisee network to get used to a structured approach and consistent effort, because this is what is expected from them. Plan your agenda in advance and share it with your network or franchisee committee before the event so that they can contribute and add topics of discussion if needed. This will promote inclusivity and make them feel heard.

Fantastic reputation

Consider appointing a person from your team whose role would be to look after the online reputation of your franchise brand. That person should possess customer service skills and understand the importance of client satisfaction. Make a plan on how to collect positive client feedback and reviews of your business and what platforms should those be on. Consider all possible channels where clients can review your services – Google My Business, Facebook, Trustpilot, Feefo, Checkatrade, etc.

Think about the specialist help you may need to implement this. Add the resources you'd need to the list of talent you started building earlier. If you cannot set this up internally, seek freelance help or an agency to help you.

Full funnel

Next, think about the areas you'd like to expand into. Where you would like to sign your next few franchisees? Why? Mapping tools and marketing intelligence would help here, so that you can carefully plan the territorial division of your franchise. Mapping tools give you a good indication of customer and regional data, demographics, competition, and much more. You could use a digital agency to perform in-depth research about how many of your potential customers search for your services online, how often they do that, and what search queries they use on Google. This will give you further indication of the market potential.

Once you have a solid plan, you should execute a lead generation campaign. This is the part of the model implementation where you will most likely need external help. This can be a team of freelancers or an agency, but it is important to remember that when you are spending money on paid ads or any form of lead generation, it is best to hire a professional who has done it before rather than experiment with your budget on an internally led campaign.

What looks like the cheaper option often works out a lot more expensive in the long run. Trying to build campaigns yourself and learning how Google, Facebook or other advertising platforms work will take a lot of time and energy, and you will probably end up wasting your budget. Do not be lured by the short-term saving. Think about your one-year and three-year plans and what the most effective way to get there is. Using specialists will guarantee you a steady lead flow and a full funnel.

If you are just starting out and have severe budget constraints, platforms like Fiverr or Upwork offer professional design, development, digital marketing and lead generation help paid by the hour. Regardless of whether you need a landing page designed and built, or some Google Ads campaigns launched, you can find cost-effective work from around the globe. You will benefit from the flexibility of working with a team without the burden of hiring anyone on a payroll, though I strongly recommend considering the help of an agency too.

Finding the fit

Last but not least, to make sure you find the right fit for your franchise every time, you will need to revise the lead qualification and onboarding processes. Now is the time to build them from scratch if, so far, you haven't had any solid processes in place. Design the journey of a potential franchisee once they have expressed their interest in learning more about the opportunity. Consider what you would like to know about them to confirm them as a suitable candidate. In return, think about what information you are comfortable disclosing about your business at the first stage of the lead qualification process. Gather all the information in a beautifully designed brochure that you can send to your candidates after the initial introductory call.

There really isn't a right or wrong way to design your qualification process, as long as you take the candidate through a series of steps where both of you learn more about each other's ambitions and expectations. Divide your requirements into 'must-haves' and 'should-haves'. This will help you cover a minimum set of requirements at the initial introductory call.

Do not forget, though, that you are looking for a business partner, and partnership is a two-way thing. You need to carefully pick the candidate, but at the same time make sure that they choose your franchise as the best opportunity for them. Attraction should be mutual.

The support a franchisee receives after the onboarding process can make or break a deal. This is why continuous training and learning should be part of the support package you provide to your network. Potential franchise partners are likely to enquire about this as part of their decision whether to invest in your franchise or one of your competitor's.

Why not collect feedback from your existing franchisees on whether your training programme can be improved? Consider how often it is revised, what new modules you can add to it, and so on. How about offering refresher sessions every six months or every year?

Have you also considered the use of mystery shoppers to visit and measure the level of customer service in different franchise locations? That can be the first step in assessing whether training is needed throughout the network or only at specific locations. The options are endless, and you can do anything, as long as you keep at the heart of your process that the ongoing training of your franchisees is to ensure the high level of customer service and incremental growth you need to improve your overall business performance.

Evaluating your success

After applying the Five Fs model, you will need to periodically evaluate it to make sure it works and delivers results. This can be done by defining clear key performance indicators for each of the Five Fs, to be measured on a regular basis. Setting clear goals for your team to aim for will not only give them clear guidance and direction, but will also serve as a benchmark when evaluating their performance later on.

Regular checks on your online reputation score should only reveal improvement. Collecting ten positive reviews from customers or improving your overall franchise brand review score from 3 to 3.5 stars, for example, are clear, quantifiable targets that can be measured. Monitoring the online reputation of each franchisee and the ratio of positive to negative reviews they receive monthly, quarterly or annually can also provide a professional key performance indicator.

A franchisor can set a number of KPIs for each franchisee. Some ideas to consider are:

- Amount of sales revenue

- Percentage of customer retention

- Amount of gross profit

- Number of complaints

- Customer satisfaction rates

- Employee satisfaction rates

You could use a robust system that collects and measures the data. It doesn't matter what KPIs you use – it really depends on what is important for you as a brand so that your KPIs align with your brand values.

Having clear objectives for your franchisees is essential for their performance too. Most franchisors go one step further and incentivise top-performing franchisees with awards and recognitions at national events and gala dinners. Whatever you decide, a minimum standard should be set for all, and if a franchisee falls below that threshold, it should trigger your training and support process.

Revisiting your lead generation strategy and measuring the number of leads you get in your sales funnel is a must too. You will probably receive monthly (if not weekly) reports on the number of leads you generate from each campaign. It is a good idea to revise your strategy every three to six months. Having in mind the number of leads per month you'd like is essential before you assign the task to an agency or your marketing manager. But what if you don't know how many leads you need in your pipeline? If you know your conversion rate, it will be easy to reverse-engineer the number.

Let's say your conversion rate is 5%, which means that for every 100 leads you get, you will sell five franchise units. If you are aiming to sell five franchises every six months, this means that you will need 100 leads during that time, or roughly 16–17 leads per month.

Those 16–17 leads should go through the qualification process, which will be improved organically over and over again. With time, you will spot gaps in the process or you will be asked questions by potential franchisees that you did not previously think of, and you will incorporate them in your starter pack. You might notice that once you have an introductory call, a lot of the leads drop out from the sales funnel and do not show interest in proceeding to the second stage. That is a clear signal that something is wrong. Or, for example, if people do not turn up for their introductory call, you might find it useful to send them a text and email reminder a couple of hours before the call to increase turn-up rate. Your lead qualification process will be refined multiple times. Regardless, I strongly recommend staying on top of the numbers ie, how many leads enter stage one of the process, how many continue to stage two, and so on. CRM systems can help you monitor the numbers.

Revisit the model

How often you should revisit the model depends on the individual performance of your franchise. But I recommend coming back to it at least once every six months to make sure that you are not missing anything. Quite often, franchisors get overwhelmed by the process of implementation and focus more on certain elements from each of the Five Fs, while omitting others. As we have discussed, the model only works when it is applied integrally rather than partially. The Five Fs form a holistic franchise marketing strategy that will help you grow your franchise not only quickly, but also sustainably.

Your business is dynamic and in constant change and development. This means that you may have to reapply or adapt the model so that it serves its purpose at certain stages of your growth. For example, when you are just starting out with one pilot or a couple of franchisees, it is a lot easier to make sure that you stay on top of your reputation and to support your franchisee team with local marketing. You would probably only need a marketing manager part-time for a day or two per week, and maybe not have an ops manager. But when your network grows to dozens, it starts to take up a lot more of your resources. It requires careful monitoring of performance, defined KPIs, minimum performance standards, and so on. You also need more help to run the franchise on a day-to-day basis, and prioritise and delegate more often. On top of that, your requirements for an ideal franchisee candidate may change a few times, which means you also need to

127

update your ideal buyer persona and, quite possibly, your qualification process.

Bear in mind that none of the tasks you set yourself to complete will yield results right away. Improving your reputation will take time. Sourcing and recruiting the best talent for all the work you have in front of you will too, and so will improving your marketing strategy to support your network of franchisees. Change does not happen overnight. But one thing is sure. The first step of this journey is the hardest – and if you are reading this book, you have already made that step. The shift in your mindset has taken place and you are now about to apply what you have learned and set off your franchise on the road to fame.

THE FIVE FS CHECKLIST

I have prepared a checklist to guide you through the process of implementing and revisiting the Five Fs, which you can download from our website on www.franchisefame.com/book.

Summary

- The Five Fs of franchise marketing model works only if regarded as holistic and all parts of it are implemented in your franchise. Do not skip any of the Five Fs.

- Set clear key performance indicators (KPIs) to evaluate the implementation of each of the Five Fs.

- Revisit the model at least every six months.

- You may need to reapply and adapt some parts of the model, depending on the stage of growth your franchise is in.

- The process of change will take time.

NINE

Next Steps

By this time, you have gained a deep understanding of the five pillars of the franchise marketing model and may have already started implementing them in your company. The results will follow. Once you have set up all the changes and put in place a sustainable revision process to evaluate the model's and business's success, it is natural to think, 'What's next?'

You have a few options ahead of you, the most obvious one being to continue growing your network of franchisees and managing your franchise domestically. Another possible route to consider is going international. This chapter looks at how the Five Fs of franchise marketing can be applied on a global scale.

Going international

After reaching a certain number of territorial units in their home country, many franchises decide to grow internationally by selling the master franchise (per country) or appointing area developers. The global franchising model operates similarly to franchising locally, although a number of changes to your business need to be considered. The same goes for the Five Fs. The five pillars of the model do not change, but applied on a global scale, certain considerations need to be made.

Before you take the huge leap of going international, make sure this is what you want and not something that has been initiated by a surprise offer from a country you have never even considered expanding into. It is important that this is something you carefully plan for, and instead of shooting in random directions, that you have a list of the top countries you'd like to begin with. Your international expansion will require a lot of hard work, but first and foremost, you need to be certain that this is what you want for your brand.

Market research is essential to the success of your global expansion. Think about the countries you see your franchise being successful in and where you have already identified market potential. Research is necessary to validate your assumptions. Think about the differences those markets have from where you are based. The fact that your franchise is successful in one country does not mean that it will be as successful in another without making any changes to the model. People in different countries search for and buy products and services in a different way, so adapting your business to the local market is critical. Alternatively, you may find that the markets are not that different and few, if any, changes to the product offering are needed.

Last, consider the legal aspects of going international. Differences in the way your company is legally allowed to operate can influence your business processes and operations. For example, employment law and taxation vary dramatically from one country to another. Make sure that you will not be unpleasantly surprised by the local regulations and consult with a legal advisor in that territory about the implications of opening up in that market.

The model at scale

Fantastic reputation

What implications does going global have on your reputation? To begin with, your record has to be spotless. Imagine the scenario where a potential master franchisor is considering investing in your business. Your numbers look great on paper, you have built a rapport with them over a number of conference calls and meetings, and you're getting ready to sign on the dotted line. They decide to do some digging before they commit and find a number of negative client reviews. Not only that, but there has been some bad press about the brand and its performance in your founding country. They back out and you're back to square one.

I have come across a case like this in my career where a media outlet has written an unflattering article about a franchise based on some ex-franchisee claims, and that article stuck to the brand like an annoying piece of chewing gum they stepped in on a hot summer day. At first the franchisor didn't think it was an issue, but every time someone looked up their brand, this article was one of the top results. How much did that article cost them in the long run, do you reckon? And would you commit to investing in that franchise if you were in the shoes of a potential master franchise buyer and you read that article? It would at least make you consider your options, right?

Franchisee network

Once you have jumped on the franchise international train, you will be looking to create a network of master franchisors, or masters in short. Much like with your franchisees, you need to support that group of master franchisors not just when opening their pilot store and making it profitable as a concept proof, but also throughout the new business development and franchisee recruitment in that country.

The lessons you have learned can be applied globally. Think about vendors that they can use cross-country to make sure you stay consistent with the quality of products and services your network receives. Introductions to a global supply chain can be incredibly valuable for your domestic business, too.

CASE STUDY – UNIFIED MARKETING DELIVERY

My agency has partnered with a global franchisor that has presence on five continents and 1500+ locations globally, and we have worked closely with them for more than seven years now. Because of that partnership, we have been able to offer to their entire network of master franchises unified and extremely competitive marketing rates. Once a new territory is sold and a master franchise is secured, we are introduced to them and present a price list for the entire network to the master franchisor. From that, they can pick and mix marketing services, such as web design and development, localising content to adapt to the local market, launching local marketing campaigns to support the pilot store launch, and developing local franchisee recruitment campaigns. This partnership guarantees consistency of the brand across all new countries while delivering high-quality digital marketing services at competitive rates.

Imagine the flip side, where each master franchisor decided to use a local provider to save costs. The output would be different from country to country and it would be incredibly difficult for the global headquarters to deliver consistent quality and high performance throughout the network.

Buying a master franchise is a big commitment, not only from an investment standpoint, but also in terms of the effort that the master franchisor will have to invest to develop the brand in the new territory. This means that their need for your strategic support will be much higher than a local franchisee's. Plan the resources they'll need and what you can do to help them grow. Try to remember what your challenges were when you first started, and the type of resources you wished you'd had.

To ensure that the master franchisors are successful, set clear targets. These can be KPIs or you could work with them to create a five-year business plan. Based on that, you can set up quantifiable targets for the end of year one, year three and year five, and measure the master franchisor's performance based on those. Their break-even point should be one of those first KPIs too. Monitoring and supporting them closely through their first months and year of business operation will minimise the risk of them failing or not hitting their targets on time. Regular accountability calls and onsite visits are good practice to keep informed and to provide timely support and advice.

Focused team

The importance of your team when going global has never been so high. Make sure you have surrounded yourself with A-players who are prepared to work flexible shifts and unusual hours. Going international means that you need to adapt to the working hours of your master franchisors. This often means starting work early or finishing late. Having such expectations of your team is OK if you carefully discuss and negotiate this with them.

Now is the time to consider the language or cultural differences in the new markets you are setting foot in. Recruiting someone who understands or has had previous experience in those markets is a good idea. In a post-pandemic world, remote teams are more widely used and accepted, so your global franchising team does not necessarily have to be located where you are. But this does mean that you need to step up your game managing the distant team. Every team member should be clear on their role and what is expected from them. On the plus side, working with distant teams can be much more cost-effective and efficient, in terms of the way they build relationships with your master franchisors and support them. Each team member should be allocated a number of masters to work with, to look after their development, progress and performance against pre-set KPIs.

Your master franchise support team will be the first point of contact for masters when they have a question or come across a challenge they cannot overcome by themselves. Make sure you have recruited people who know your business and franchise well enough and have the necessary business skills and integrity to be of assistance. Those skills can be trained, but it is also good practice to promote someone internally who has been with you for a while and knows all the processes of the business.

Full funnel

Master franchise lead generation is as important as any other point of the model, if not more. Finding the right candidate who can afford to buy the licence for the territory and who possesses the necessary skills to grow the brand can be a challenging task, which can take some time. It starts with defining your buyer persona again, as you have done when generating local franchise recruitment leads. But the ideal master franchise avatar will be quite different.

Think about the qualities a successful candidate should possess – years of business experience, their level in previous organisations, and so forth. As a general rule, the higher the investment and responsibility, the more experienced and senior profile you will be looking for. It is an advantage if they have expertise and experience in the same sector, but anyone senior enough who has led a business to growth and national/international expansion should be high on your list.

Do not get discouraged if the process takes longer than expected. Hunting for master franchise leads usually takes longer than any other lead generation you have previously done. You may want to test different audiences if the one you have already tried does not bring results. Sometimes you may even be too specific about the person you are looking for, so broadening your target audience can be a good idea. Always start wider and then keep refining until you find that sweet spot of candidates who fit your ideal master franchisor profile.

Another common way to generate leads is through using a local representative. If you know someone based in the local market, it is a good idea to incentivise them to serve as your local representative. If they generate leads for you and one successfully signs a master franchise agreement, they receive a certain pre-agreed commission, usually equal to the cost that you would have spent on a marketing campaign for the same result.

In terms of campaigns, localise your messages as much as possible. This means trying to understand the differences of the target market/country and adapting to them. When searching for a master franchisor for a particular country, the language you should use for all your marketing is English, as this is the international business language. After all, as a very minimum, you'd want your masters to have good command of English for business correspondence and communication. When I speak about differences, it is the cultural ones that I refer to. For example, the way you do business in the Middle East is very different from Japan.

The opportunity has to be presented in a clear and comprehensive way. From experience, a separate landing page for each market/country works best. Provide as much detail as possible about why you are certain that your franchise would be successful in the local market. Give information about your business and the opportunity, and potentially some case studies of other countries and territories where you have replicated the business model successfully. You can also add information such as who your ideal candidate is and what qualities they should possess. It is a good idea to include an FAQ section for potential candidates.

The page should also consist of a lead magnet – an action the user can take so that you capture their personal information. This can be downloading a brochure about the opportunity with extra information on the investment, for example, or filling out a form to request more information or schedule a conference call with your team. It is important to note that you should use business language throughout all communication with any potential leads, whether verbal, written, on your website and in marketing collateral.

Setting up the correct tracking is of paramount importance to the success of the campaign. If you are running campaigns on different channels, such as LinkedIn, Facebook, Google Ads, etc, you need to know which is the most successful and cost-effective channel. LinkedIn is usually the first channel you should think of when selling master franchise opportunities, but again, this depends on the market and country. Other channels should be tested to make sure. Implementing the right tracking methods can be quite a technical task, so do make sure you have the right team member for that or hire someone external.

You shouldn't be hoping for a high number of leads. Your funnel can be full with only one or two serious candidates per country/territory. Do not expect the same level of lead flow as selling franchises locally. The master franchisor opportunity is exclusive and only suitable for a handful of people.

To summarise, the main difference between launching a local franchise recruitment campaign and a global one is the type of buyer persona you will be looking to attract. By extension, this means you'll have different target audiences for your lead generation campaigns.

Finding the fit

As we have looked at above, searching for a global partner will not be as easy as finding local franchisees. But do not be discouraged – you can replicate your local model on an international scale and adapt it where needed. Make sure you know who you are looking for specifically, as well as what information you are ready to put on the table.

The lead qualification process here will look more like a negotiation than a job interview. Yes, you must make sure you are picking the right candidate for the opportunity. But you want to make sure they pick you in return. If a businessperson or organisation is ready to invest in your franchise and buy exclusivity to operate in a country under your trademark, they have probably done this before, or are currently running a successful business and looking to differentiate their portfolio. You should approach the conversation with the understanding that they do not need you, but you would mutually benefit from a business relationship.

Only after making that shift in mindset can you start designing your qualification process so that you disclose the right information at every step of the way. Make sure the initial introduction is based on getting to know each other – your experience, aspirations, drive. Take the opportunity to present your franchise as candidly as you can. You do not want to oversell it. The person in front of you will know if you are sugar-coating your story.

Check any local legislation with a legal advisor and whether the shortlisted candidates meet the requirements. Make sure your contracts are valid internationally and meet the local regulations. When you get to the final stage of signing the agreement and receiving a deposit for the deal, you do not want to be disrupted by a rookie glitch in the contract or a clause that does not hold in court.

Draw up a plan of revenue streams for your potential master franchisor to make your value offering higher. Include a few options, such as owning a series of franchise locations themselves, as well as selling franchise units. If the country they are buying a franchise for is big enough, why not consider selling to area franchisors, who then do the local franchise recruitment themselves. Lay out all opportunities to get your future partners excited about investing in a master franchise with you.

When negotiating and meeting your potential international business partners, be considerate of cultural differences. As much as business is done similarly across the globe and the basic principles of economics and finance are universally valid, the language barrier, the difference in cultures, time difference and other factors must be taken into account when preparing to meet and converse with businesspeople from other countries, ethnic backgrounds and origins. This might not be a factor when you are expanding to neighbouring countries or within the same continent, but may play a critical role when you are building relationships with potential partners from somewhere afar.

CASE STUDY – JAPAN

This reminds me of a business meeting I had to attend in Tokyo a few years back. I had to present the agency's services to a master franchisor there, and the introduction was made by their headquarters in Europe. Luckily, I knew that the way business is done in Japan is very traditional and follows an almost ceremonial flow – introduction, exchange of business cards, bows, etc. The day before the meeting, I read as much information online about dos and don'ts, and the most common mistakes people make. That helped ease any initial tension. It also made a positive impression on the hosts, who were delighted to see that I had taken the meeting seriously and respectfully prepared for it according to the local customs. The presentation and conversation flowed easily.

International training

Your master franchisor's success will depend on how well they understand your franchise model and apply it in the new territory. As such, their training plan has to be adapted to the conditions of the local market, but must also encompass the various parts of the business, such as marketing and finance, sales, supply chain and management, and so forth. It is a mini MBA studied through the prism of your franchise, and should summarise the lessons you have learned throughout your franchising journey.

Various people from your organisation should teach the training modules. It can be a good idea to involve partners and even other master franchisors in the training process, so that they can receive hands-on experience and training from peers. The length of the whole process may take a couple of weeks to a few months, depending on the locations involved, the length of modules, etc. Usually, the training is done at your headquarters so international travel is also involved if the conditions allow it.

Once you have decided to embark on your international expansion journey, stay attentive, and follow what you already know – because you know your franchise best. Remember, the world is your oyster. Good luck!

Summary

- First, make sure international expansion is what you really want.

- The Five Fs of franchise marketing are applicable at the global scale, but certain factors need to be kept in mind.

- Market research is crucial. Test any theories you have properly before going ahead.

- Your reputation has to be spotless.

- Prepare your team of A-players and get their buy-in to provide support to international partners.

- Strategy and execution should always be adapted to the target market, taking into consideration the socio-economical, demographic and cultural differences.

- Recruiting master franchisors is very different from local franchisee recruitment and takes time and effort.

- Adapt your buyer persona and your lead generation processes to attract the best international partner for your business.

- Plan comprehensive training and deliver it with the help of an international team of peers and internal experts.

Conclusion

Congratulations on completing this book! I sincerely wish you best of luck with growing your franchise, achieving soaring success and finding franchise fame. Although I am sure that if you follow the Five Fs of franchise marketing, you will not be needing any luck at all.

You will have, by now, picked up on the main message of the book. Namely, that every chapter of the model is related to a participating party in your franchise. Only by managing all stakeholders collectively, through aligning their goals with the overall business objectives, will you hit your ambitious targets and even exceed your own expectations.

People are at the core of your business. Building the right relationships with your team and creating a company people would love to work in, while carefully selecting and supporting your partners old and new, provide the right formula for success. There is no quick and easy way. We should not forget the vendors and end clients of your brand, without whom the business would not even exist. Successful relationships are what successful franchising is all about.

If you would like to know more about how to begin implementing the Five Fs, there is a wealth of information on our website www.franchisefame.com.

As a small gift to you, I have made available our Five Fs of Franchise Marketing measurement tool so you can start implementing the model straightaway. After answering a series of questions about your business, the tool will create a custom report to allow you to improve all areas of your franchise business. The tool can be found on our website www.franchisefame.com/scorecard.

Acknowledgements

I would like to thank all clients and partners of the agency over the years, as well as the ones mentioned in the book as examples and case studies. You have contributed towards years of experience and learning that I am extremely grateful for and that I am happy to now be sharing with others.

I'd like to also thank my business partners, mentors and dear friends Anton Skarlatov and Rune Sovndahl. Because of them, I am the person I am today. They gave me a chance at the earliest stage of my career and have, since then, continuously believed in me and encouraged me to be exceptional throughout my journey. You both mean so much to me.

Huge thanks to Carla van Wyk, Clayton Treloar, Jenny Farenden, Clive Smith, Jennifer Hadjieva and Polina Peycheva for their contribution and invaluable feedback. You are all key people in your industries and I appreciate your time and support.

I am also very proud of and indebted to my team of extremely skilful individuals who have supported me along the way. Without you, none of this would have been possible. In particular: our Marketing Operations Manager, Rosen Dinev; Account Director, Iva Dimitrova; Head of Sales, Antonia Georgieva; and very talented designer, Desislava Ruseva.

Finally, I'd also like to thank God. I stay humble and extremely grateful for all the blessings that He has sent my way.

Thank you, all!

The Author

 Dani holds a BSc in Business Management and Economics and an MSc in Strategic Project Management from University College London. She started her career as a Brand Manager client-side before moving to found the agency Local Fame and, later, Franchise Fame. Ever since, she has worked in branding and digital and franchise marketing with clients from around the globe.

Dani has been interviewed and featured in multiple media outlets. Her extensive experience in business and franchising, client- and agency-side, has given her valuable expertise in the industry. Dani has also been a guest speaker at multiple events, on podcasts and at conferences around the world, sharing her insights on franchise marketing. She is available for talks and interviews upon request.

If you'd like to discuss your franchise marketing needs or need help implementing any part of the model in the book, please contact Dani at office@franchisefame.com to schedule a call.

For more detailed information on what we do, please check out our website: www.franchisefame.com

And connect with us on social media at:

f www.facebook.com/Franchise-Fame-101504668836553

in www.linkedin.com/company/franchise-fame

t https://twitter.com/famefranchise

o www.instagram.com/franchisefame

▶ https://bit.ly/3Lqqcik